HEALING YOUR ALONENESS

HEALING YOUR ALONENESS

Finding Love and Wholeness Through Your Inner Child

ERIKA J. CHOPICH, Ph.D.

AND

MARGARET PAUL, Ph.D.

HarperSanFrancisco

A Division of HarperCollins*Publishers*

To contact Dr. Erika Chopich or Dr. Margaret Paul for information regarding lectures and workshops, or free copies of the charts in this book, please write to 2531 Sawtelle Boulevard, #42, Los Angeles, CA 90064.

Library of Congress Cataloging-in-Publication Data
Chopich, Erika J.
    Healing your aloneness : finding love and wholeness through your inner
child / Erika J. Chopich, Margaret Paul.
        p.   cm.
    ISBN 0-06-250149-6
    1. Loneliness. 2. Self. I. Paul, Margaret. II. Title.
III. Title: Inner child.
BF575.L7C55   1990
158′.2—dc20   89-46151
                                                                                    CIP

   91 92 93 94   VICKS   10 9 8 7 6 5 4

To the memory of my aunt, Lucille Ralph,
a World War II veteran,
whose childlike spirit is with me always.

And to Danielle Ray my "adopted"
daughter whose courageous
spirit helps my loving Adult to grow.

Erika J. Chopich

To my parents, Charlotte and Izzy Brustein,
and to my aunt, Anne Louis,
for their devoted love and support.

Margaret Paul

Contents

Preface

Every self-help book poses the same questions: Why are there so many unhappy marriages? Why is there so much crime and violence and hatred? Why is there so much tension, anxiety, and illness? Why is there so much child abuse? Why are there so many unhappy people, people in pain, people with low self-esteem, people who feel alone and empty?

Our culture is rampant with people who are addicted to something—alcohol, drugs, food, cigarettes, work, TV, money, power, relationships, religion, approval, caretaking, sex, affection, romance—all ways to get filled up from outside of ourselves.

Why? Why are we so empty within that we continually look for new ways to fill ourselves from outside? What has happened in our society that has led to such emptiness?

Our society is in a deep spiritual crisis, a crisis that is the result of having taken the wrong path thousands of years ago. We are experiencing the consequences of the internal disconnection from our own hearts that began even before the birth of Christ.

The natural human state is a heart that is filled to the brim with love and light, so full that it overflows and pours out love and light with every breath. But so many of us are far away from that natural state, so far away that all we feel is a sense of emptiness in our hearts. And when our hearts are empty, and when we don't know how to fill them from the inside, then we are left trying to fill them from the outside. That's what addiction and codependence is all about—trying to fill oneself up from the outside.

Our world is at a crossroads. We are each being challenged to choose between love, peace, and life, or fear, war, and death. We have achieved much on this planet, but at what price? With all we have achieved, we are still left with polluted water and air, wars, hunger, crime, fear, and misery. What has gone wrong? What is missing in the world as a whole, and in our relationships, our families, and within ourselves?

The survival of our planet depends on all of us understanding and experiencing that we are all one. When we can look at other human beings and feel a sense of unity, then we can no longer violate each other physically or emotionally. This feeling of unity with all of life will not be achieved until we feel unified within ourselves. Our sense of isolation and loneliness can only be transcended through experiencing inner wholeness and connection.

We feel alone when we disconnect from ourselves, and then we feel lonely because we cannot connect to others until we connect to ourselves. This book is about understanding how we got so disconnected from ourselves and how we can reconnect and learn to fill ourselves up from the inside. It is about how we cause our own emptiness and aloneness and how we can create our own fullness. It is about how we learned to abandon ourselves and what we must do to love ourselves. It is when we love ourselves that our hearts fill up and the love overflows to others. We cannot love others any more than we love ourselves, and we cannot receive others' love until we receive our own.

Acknowledgments

We want to thank Michael Toms, our editor, who saw the value in our book and brought us to Harper & Row.

We want to thank Drs. David and Rebecca Grudermeyer and Jackie Benster for reading the manuscript and offering many helpful comments.

We want to thank Sheryl Paul and Danielle Ray for reading the manuscript and putting it into practice in their own lives.

Most of all we want to thank our clients, who have shared themselves with us, have allowed us to use their sessions as examples, and have written special pieces for this book.

Introduction

This book is about the Inner Child inside every human being and about the need to connect that Child with its loving Inner Adult. Coauthor Erika Chopich describes below her own experience of her Inner Child and Adult.

There isn't anybody I know who hasn't felt really alone and lonely at one time or another. Some people seem to have a chronic, nagging feeling of inner aloneness. Others are in a constant state of conflict in their relationships, either pulling at each other to take away their feeling of loneliness, or trying to make sure that they will not be left alone. It seems that everybody deals with feelings of aloneness and loneliness much of the time. It may be that all of the books, workshops, and psychotherapies are really designed to do just one thing: help us feel connected so that we don't feel alone.

I had a very difficult and isolated childhood but overcame feelings of aloneness early by adopting my Inner Child. I always wondered why people would rather feel alone than talk to their Inner Child.

During one of my women's groups we were talking about listening to your Inner Child. I had only alluded to it when one woman, Charlene, pressed me for more information. She wanted to know exactly what I meant by "Inner Child" and by the connection between the "Inner Adult and the Inner Child" and was relentless in her pursuit of further understanding. It was Charlene's insistence, openness, and dedication to her growth that prompted me to describe for the first time something that I thought all people did naturally.

I have always had loving inner dialogues between my Adult and my Child. Even as a small child I can remember my Adult consulting my Child about what she wanted and needed and my Child consulting my Adult about understanding external matters and how to do things in the world. My inner process was so natural to me, even though I had not labeled it until recently as Adult and Child, that it never occurred to me that everyone else did not have the same inner process.

I explained my inner dialogues to Charlene and described the dialogues that I held aloud when I felt stressed. As I talked about the feeling of love and trust that exists between my Adult and Child, the group began to get excited.

Charlene kept asking me more and more questions; as I gave the answers something new began to happen within the group.

Coauthor Margaret Paul describes how she first learned about Erika's experience of her Inner Child and Adult and the effect on her of that discovery.

I have spent my life on an inward spiritual search. My goals have been to be a loving human being and to find inner joy and peace.

I am a psychotherapist, and I have developed a form of therapy which I call Intention Therapy. Intention Therapy is based on the theory that there are only two basic intentions in life—the intent to protect and the intent to learn. Most of us, especially when we feel discomfort, pain, or fear, have learned to protect against knowing about, experiencing, and taking responsibility for these feelings. We protect by disconnecting from these feelings in various ways. The intent to protect keeps us locked into behaving in ways that perpetuate the very fear and pain we are trying to avoid.

When I discovered some years ago that we have another choice, that is, the choice to learn from our pain and fear and thus find ways out of these feelings, I began an intensive process within myself. And I was successful to a certain extent. I felt more powerful within and more able to be consistently loving to others. But something was still missing. I still felt alone inside some of the time, and I often felt alone around others. I still wasn't feeling the deep peace and joy that I knew was possible and that I occasionally felt, and try as I might I couldn't figure out what was wrong.

Then Erika talked to me one day after one of her women's groups. She said, "Something happened in group today, and I'm feeling excited about it. Charlene started to question me about my internal process, and I got into describing the connection between my Adult and my Child. The group was blown away by it."

As Erika described what she had told the group, I felt a quiver of excitement. Yes! Oh yes! There was something very exciting here! Everything within me came alive, and I knew that she had discovered something wonderful, although it took me another week to fully understand what she was talking about and comprehend the power of it. I had known about and had done "inner child work"—learning about the feelings I had as a child and attempting to heal them through others' love—but what Erika was talking about was different. She was talking about an inner loving relationship, what we've now come to call *Inner Bonding Therapy.*

For some time now I've been working deeply with my loving Inner Adult and Inner Child, and everything in my life has changed. As a result of truly listening to my Inner Child and being loving to her, I realized that I was still playing the role of caretaker in my marriage and that it was making me very unhappy and leaving me feeling constantly drained and ill. When I finally

pulled back from that role, my marriage went into turmoil and eventually separation. My marriage and an intact family has been very important to me, so
this change is very difficult, yet I've never been happier in my life. People who
haven't seen me for a while tell me that I look radiant, and I feel radiant within
myself much of the time. I've found the missing peace that I've sought for so
long, and it's so exciting.

Understanding that the intent to learn is basic to any growth has been very
important to me, but it was not enough. Understanding that the intent to learn
means *learning from and with the Inner Child and taking responsibility for all the
feelings of the Inner Child* has made all the difference. We can intend to learn
about the world. We can intend to learn about another person. But until we
intend to learn with and from our Inner Child, we will not heal our inner
isolation nor become whole.

Part 1

UNDERSTANDING THE INNER CHILD AND ADULT

CHAPTER 1

You Have an Inner Child

All the people we call "geniuses" are men and women who somehow escaped having to put that curious, wondering child in themselves to sleep.

Wishcraft
BARBARA SHER

All of us have two distinct aspects of our personality: the Adult and the
Child. When these two parts are connected and working together,
there is a sense of wholeness within. When these two parts are disconnected, however, because of being wounded, dysfunctional, or
undeveloped, there is a sense of conflict, emptiness, and aloneness
within.

It is very important to have a clear and positive understanding of
the Inner Child. Traditionally in our culture children have been seen as
less than adults—less important and less knowing. As children we
generally experienced ourselves as powerless, so we often equate the
concepts of powerlessness and unimportance with being a child. In
addition, because we were so often told that we were bad and the cause
of trouble, we may think of our Inner Child as a troublemaker. Because
we were not truly valued as children, it may be hard to value the Child
within us. We may discount its importance, thereby perpetuating our
experiences of childhood by creating a disconnection within ourselves
that then causes our misery. Understanding and valuing our Child is
essential for becoming whole.

Defining the Inner Child

The Inner Child has a full range of intense emotions—joy and pain,
happiness and sadness. The Inner Child functions in the right-brain
modes of *being, feeling, and experiencing,* as opposed to the Adult who
functions in the left-brain modes of *doing, thinking, and acting,* but who
also has a full range of feelings. "Doing" relates to the external physical

world and to performing an action, while "being" refers to existing on an internal, emotional, and spiritual level. "Doing" is an outer experience while "being" is an inner experience.

Here is an example in Erika's words of how she comforted her Inner Child during a sudden and intense moment of grief.

How we really function became very clear to me on a trip to San Diego that a friend and I had taken. We went to Sea World to see the new Orca calf that had just been born. While we were watching the baby whale I began searching the tank for my friend Orky, a large male killer whale that I had become acquainted with. I loved Orky and knew him on sight, but I couldn't find him in the tank.

All of a sudden a chill swept over me when I saw divers leaving a holding tank in the back of the stadium. I knew Orky was dead. We frantically ran to the other side of the tank and asked the trainers what had happened. They told us nothing was wrong—they pointed to a small female whale and told me that was Orky. I knew better. My fears became real after talking to one of the divers.

I immediately felt stunned with grief and sadness. Both parts of me were sad and crying, but each part of me experienced that grief from a different place. The Adult part of me was not only sad, but outraged. I was angry that I had been lied to and concerned with the kind of care Orky had been given. My first impulse from my Adult was to *do* something, to search out someone in authority and demand an explanation. Then I heard the voice of my Inner Child. She didn't care about who was involved or about how and why it had happened—she was in too much pain for anger. She only knew she had lost her big friend and would never see him again. She felt awful that they wouldn't even let her say goodbye.

I decided my first responsibility was to my Inner Child and before I would do anything else I would let her *be* and deal with her grief first. So we sat on a bench and sobbed for several minutes. I was glad that I made the decision to let my investigations wait until she was ready. Had I not allowed her that time and experience, my grief would have been much more difficult for me to deal with. My Inner Child would have felt not only the loss of Orky, but the loss of my caring as well.

The Child is the instinctual part of us, our "gut" feelings. The Child has sometimes been referred to as the unconscious, but it is unconscious only because we have paid so little attention to it. The unconscious becomes readily available to consciousness when we wish to learn about it. Our Inner Child contains our feelings, memories, and experiences from childhood, which can be remembered when we seek to learn from our Inner Child.

We can look at the Child in two distinct ways—the Child when it is being loved by the Inner Adult and the Child when it is unloved, when it is criticized, neglected, and abandoned by the Inner Adult. There is only one Inner Child. At any given moment that Child is either being loved or unloved by the Inner Adult, and its feelings and behavior come directly from the Adult's choice to learn about the Child's wants, needs, and feelings and take responsibility for them, or to protect against this knowing and responsibility.

The Unloved Child

When the Inner Adult chooses to protect him/herself against experiencing and being responsible for the feelings and needs of the Child, then the Adult disconnects from the Child through various forms of shaming, neglect, and indulgence. The Child is left feeling unloved, abandoned, and very much alone inside. The Child concludes that it must be bad, wrong, unlovable, unimportant, inadequate, or not enough, or it would not have been abandoned, originally by external adults (parents and grandparents) and eventually by the Inner Adult. The external and internal disconnections create intense fear, guilt, and shame within the Child, and feelings of being alone in the world and alone inside. The Child learns to fear being rejected, abandoned, and controlled, first by external caretakers and then by the Inner Adult, and eventually projects these fears onto others, generally believing that others are rejecting, abandoning, or attempting to control him or her.

The feeling of aloneness is the hardest feeling for all of us to feel. It causes such deep pain that we all work hard to protect ourselves from feeling it. When parents and other adults reject, shame, abandon, and abuse us as children, the pain of their abandonment is so unbearable that the Inner Adult disconnects from the Inner Child so as not to experience these feelings. Then the Inner Child not only feels alone and lonely in the world, but feels alone and empty inside as well, with no one inside to protect it from being hurt by others.

As we grow up, the abandoned Inner Child learns to project onto others the internal experience of abandonment. If the Inner Child feels controlled, criticized, or neglected by the Inner Adult, then it often projects this out onto others and experiences others as controlling, critical, or abandoning, whether or not this is actually happening. The anger the Inner Child feels at the Inner Adult for abandoning it is generally projected onto others. The Child comes to believe that the abandonment is only external because the Child has no way to express its anger to the Inner Adult. The unloving Inner Adult is unavailable to hearing the feelings of the Inner Child. The anger and blame we feel toward others as adults is not only a projection onto others of the external parental rejection, but of the internal abandonment as well.

The abandoned Inner Child is constantly afraid of being wrong because it believes that being wrong is what leads to rejection. Therefore, it strives to find the "right" way to be in the world. It becomes addicted to "shoulds" and rules as a way to control rejection. It develops a need to be perfect and a belief that it is possible to be perfect. Perfectionism and the fear of being wrong are symptoms of the internal disconnection between the Adult and the Child.

The abandoned Inner Child, feeling desperately empty, alone, and lonely, with no Inner Adult to help handle the loneliness of external abandonment, turns to various addictions to fill itself up. This wounded, abandoned Inner Child survives the shame and pain inflicted by its primary caretakers by becoming addicted to a wide range of substances or behaviors. Anne Wilson Schaef, in *When Society Becomes an Addict*, states that 96 percent of our population suffers from substance and process addictions. Addictions to alcohol, drugs, food, sugar, caffeine, and nicotine are substance addictions. Process addictions fall into two different categories: addiction to people (codependence) and addiction to things and activities. The Inner Child can become addicted to TV, work, sports, sleep, exercise, power, money, spending, gambling, shoplifting, reading, talking, talking on the telephone, meditation, religion, drama, danger, glamor, worry, ruminating, and even to misery and depression as a way to fill the emptiness. The Inner Child turns to substances, things, and activities as an escape from the pain of external and internal aloneness and loneliness.

In addition, the Child can become addicted to a relationship, to sex, romance, love, and approval. Every Child needs approval. When it cannot get approval from the Inner Adult, then it has no choice but to try to get love and approval from others. The individual's sense of adequacy and lovability become attached to the approval of others when its Inner Adult is unloving. This is neediness—needing others to make us feel okay about ourselves. This neediness for external approval sets up deep fears of rejection and domination from those whose approval the Child wants. Approval, sex, and love become the way the Inner Child tries to escape its unbearable aloneness, *never realizing that external connection with others cannot occur without internal connection to oneself.*

When we believe that we need love, sex, or approval in order to feel okay, but inside we feel unlovable, then we believe we need to control getting that love and approval and avoiding rejection. The needy, abandoned Inner Child tries to control how others treat it and feel about it by instilling guilt and fear in them. It does this with irritation, anger, blame, silent withdrawal of love, righteousness, tantrums, violence, pouting, crying, lying, teaching, lecturing, explaining, interrogating, and/or telling feelings. The Inner Child, feeling desperately alone and lonely, is operating under a false belief. It is saying, "I can make others love me, see me, hear me, and approve of me, connect to me, and give me more of what I want. When they do, I will feel okay about myself." A desperately lonely and frightened Inner Child is often impulsive, self-involved, with little control over its behavior. The deeper the internal abandonment, the more desperate the Child is to alleviate the pain and the more it will act out in destructive and self-destructive ways. It's very important to realize that *this is not who your Inner Child really is, but who it is when it has been abandoned externally and internally.*

Another way the Inner Child may try to control is through compliance and caretaking. The Child becomes the "good" boy or girl, putting aside his or her own needs in favor of others' needs. This Child acts like an adult, taking over the job of fixing things for everyone, or becoming overly nice or seductive. When we are complying, caretaking, enabling, or pulling with niceness, we are operating under false beliefs. We are saying, "I don't count. What I want and feel is not important. Other people's wants and feelings are more important than mine. I can make people love me or approve of me by being nice or by being seductive." These are all ways that the abandoned Inner Child behaves toward others to get love and to protect itself against rejection and abandonment.

The fear of being dominated and engulfed is just as powerful as the fear of being rejected and abandoned. When this fear is activated, which may occur when someone wants control over you or wants something from you, your abandoned Inner Child protects itself through some form of resistance. Responding from your abandoned Inner Child, you may get defensive in reaction to what someone wants or feels, or you may deny what you feel, or what you've done. Or you may resort to withdrawal or indifference, losing yourself in an activity, or deadening yourself with a substance. You might become rigid in your point of view, or you might rebel and do the opposite of what the other person wants of you. Or perhaps you agree to comply but actually resist through procrastination, incompetence, or forgetting. This behavior comes from the false belief that not being controlled is more important than anything. A person with this pattern of behavior is

Inner Adult Disconnecting from Inner Child

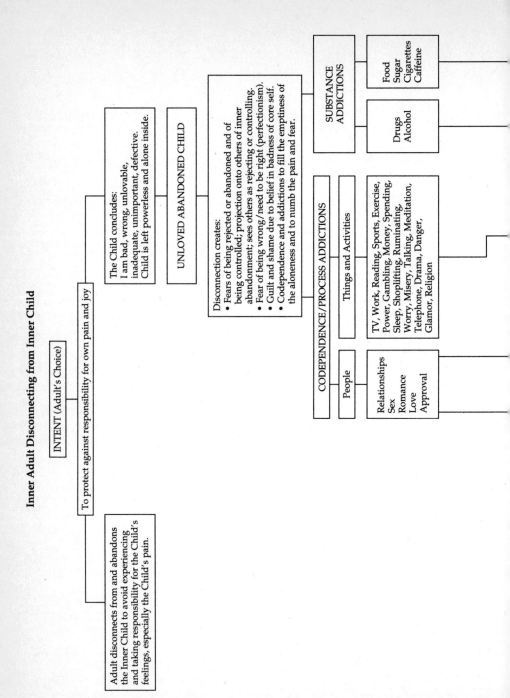

INTENT (Adult's Choice)

To protect against responsibility for own pain and joy

Adult disconnects from and abandons the Inner Child to avoid experiencing and taking responsibility for the Child's feelings, especially the Child's pain.

The Child concludes:
I am bad, wrong, unlovable, inadequate, unimportant, defective. Child is left powerless and alone inside.

UNLOVED ABANDONED CHILD

Disconnection creates:
• Fears of being rejected or abandoned and of being controlled; projection onto others of inner abandonment; sees others as rejecting or controlling.
• Fear of being wrong/need to be right (perfectionism).
• Guilt and shame due to belief in badness of core self.
• Codependence and addictions to fill the emptiness of the aloneness and to numb the pain and fear.

SUBSTANCE ADDICTIONS

Drugs
Alcohol

Food
Sugar
Cigarettes
Caffeine

CODEPENDENCE/PROCESS ADDICTIONS

People

Things and Activities

Relationships
Sex
Romance
Love
Approval

TV, Work, Reading, Sports, Exercise, Power, Gambling, Money, Spending, Sleep, Shoplifting, Ruminating, Worry, Misery, Talking, Meditation, Telephone, Drama, Danger, Glamor, Religion

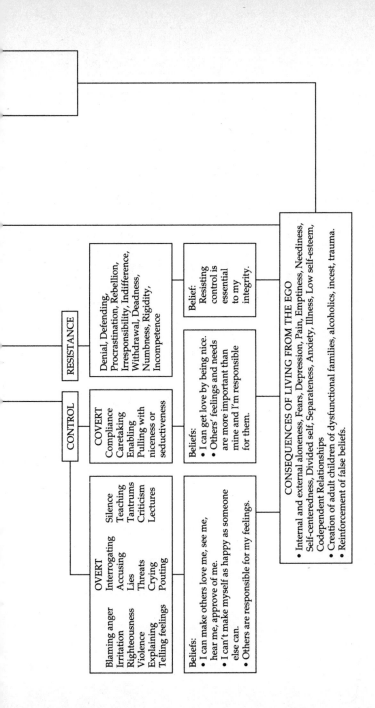

OVERT

Blaming anger
Irritation
Righteousness
Violence
Explaining
Telling feelings

Interrogating
Accusing
Lies
Threats
Crying
Pouting

Silence
Teaching
Tantrums
Criticism
Lectures

Beliefs:
• I can make others love me, see me, hear me, approve of me.
• I can't make myself as happy as someone else can.
• Others are responsible for my feelings.

CONTROL

COVERT

Compliance
Caretaking
Enabling
Pulling with niceness or seductiveness

Beliefs:
• I can get love by being nice.
• Others' feelings and needs are more important than mine and I'm responsible for them.

RESISTANCE

Denial, Defending,
Procrastination, Rebellion,
Irresponsibility, Indifference,
Withdrawal, Deadness,
Numbness, Rigidity,
Incompetence

Belief: Resisting control is essential to my integrity.

CONSEQUENCES OF LIVING FROM THE EGO
• Internal and external aloneness, Fears, Depression, Pain, Emptiness, Neediness, Self-centeredness, Divided self, Separateness, Anxiety, Illness, Low self-esteem, Codependent Relationships
• Creation of adult children of dysfunctional families, alcoholics, incest, trauma.
• Reinforcement of false beliefs.

saying, "If I do what someone else wants (even if it's something I also want) I will lose myself and my integrity." People in resistance do not decide for themselves what they want. They just resist what others want for them or from them. They are actually being controlled by their resistance, even though their resistance is intended to protect them from being controlled by others.

The abandoned Inner Child (see chart on pages 8 and 9) is doing the best it can to protect itself in the above ways, but all these protections end up creating even more external and internal aloneness.

The Loved Child

When the Child feels loved, it is the natural Child within us. It is our aliveness, enthusiasm, and sense of wonder. The loved Child within us is so special that the briefest contact with it opens us to the absolute delight of just being alive. The loved Child is energetic and filled with passion, playfulness, and curiosity, and is always receptive to new ideas and experiences. The natural Inner Child is our creativity, intuition, and ability to trust. When the Inner Child was loved as a child by its caretakers, or has been lovingly re-parented by the Inner Adult for a long time, it is soft, sensitive, flowing, and very loving. Within the loved Child lies our understanding of the inherent equality of all people and the unity of all being. The loved Child is wise and knowing in a holistic, nonlinear way, which means drawing conclusions through a totality of multiple and simultaneous experiences and impressions, rather than through step-by-step logical and linear thinking, which is the realm of the Adult.

The Child, being conceptual rather than linear, contains our ability for deep emotional and spiritual connection within ourselves and with others. It is the loved Child that can tell us what we feel and want based upon what *feels* right or wrong to it. It is the loved Child part of us that knows what is best for us, what feels good or bad to us. It is these feelings that give us accurate information about what makes us happy or unhappy. People who are out of touch with their Inner Child are out of touch with many of their feelings and have no access to this source of knowledge.

Our society has long diminished the importance of feelings, worshiping logic while downgrading the wisdom that comes from feelings, touting the left brain while ignoring the right. And this has created a terrible imbalance—the power of logic without the power of wisdom. Wisdom is the accumulation of all our experiences stored as emotion. When you cannot *feel* what is true, then you cannot utilize your wisdom.

Many people, denying their feelings and the wisdom of the Child, have tried to establish their identity through doing rather than by doing and being. Is a person's identity only connected to what he or she does? What about beingness? What about softness, tenderness, empathy, intuitiveness, awareness, and feelings? What about curiosity, spontaneity, and playfulness? We will not come into our full power and wisdom until we see that these qualities are just as important as our achievements.

The loved Child is empathic—feeling deeply into the feelings of others. It is this aspect of ourselves that wants to rescue others to relieve them of their pain. The loved Child feels pain when others are in pain and wants to do something to relieve it. The Loving Adult needs to help the Child know when this is loving and when it is enabling.

The loved Child is playful and imaginative. There is a sense of excitement and enthusiasm about people who are in contact with this fun and alive aspect of themselves. People who are connected to their Inner Child respond to life with animation and spontaneity. They are appropriately spontaneous: they are neither impulsive and out of control, nor withdrawn and inhibited.

There is a vast difference between being "childlike" (animated and spontaneous) and "childish" (impulsive and out of control). People often confuse the two, judging the spontaneous person, the playful and imaginative person who has a sense of wonder, to be immature or unsophisticated and admonishing him or her to "grow up." As a consequence, people often abandon their Inner Child, or at least try to hide it. Adults who are disconnected from their Inner Child find great difficulty in playing and having fun. To most of them, playing involves adult activities, such as going to a formal cocktail party, a fine restaurant, or a movie; watching a competitive sports event; or getting drunk or stoned.

The Inner Child is critically important to our well-being. Our ability to have fun depends on our degree of access to our Inner Child. True playing is very different than just participating in an activity, and is spontaneous rather than planned. It is an attitude that can happen anywhere. It can be experienced at the zoo or on a swing, or even just standing in line at the market or making dinner—it's there whenever we are open to our delight. It is a flowing, exhilarating feeling of joy filled with laughter. When was the last time you really let go and had fun? Very often the only time we allow this in ourselves is when we first fall in love. Somehow we can give permission to lovers to skip, swing, sing, tickle, and play like children, while the same behavior in those who are not "in love" is judged as inappropriate. Perhaps it is this very aspect of being in love that we all find so attractive and enlivening. All too soon, however, young lovers decide it is now time to be responsible (believing that means they have to ignore the Child), and they disconnect from the Child, becoming all Adult or all abandoned Child. Or their fears of rejection and control and their resulting protections take over, and they slowly disconnect from the feelings of the Child. Eventually, they find their way to our office where they complain that the life seems to have gone out of their relationship and they just don't know how to connect anymore! On occasion they will opt to go their separate ways in search of a new playmate and start the cycle all over again. This is usually not necessary if they will take responsibility for their own feelings and move into the intent to learn with their own Inner Child.

Our sensuality—the deep experience of touch, taste, smell, and hearing—belong to the Child. Children are sensual people. They experience life through their senses, and with their whole bodies. They become totally involved in every experience with a nonjudgmental innocence because they are so completely in the moment. They walk in a free, arm-swinging style and they sing when they feel like singing. They touch almost everything they see. Most importantly, though, they love to hug and be hugged! This is who *we* become whenever we connect with our Inner Child. Most of us say to ourselves, "There is a time to play and a time to work, and when it is time to play, *then* I will connect to my Inner Child." But imagine how your life would flow if you spent most of it, even work time, in a playful, creative, joyous place!

Kate, a woman in one of our groups, is one of the most delightful people we've ever known. Because she almost always exudes fun and joy, we asked her to write something for us on the Inner Child.

When Margie and Erika first suggested "playfulness" as a possible topic to write on, my heart jumped—now there's one topic I can relate to! But I almost talked myself out of writing about it, thinking that it would be more effective for someone who has struggled to regain her long lost Child to write on the subject rather than me, because my Child has pretty much dominated my personality all of my life.

When I hear others talk about giving the Child within permission to come out and play, when I see the pain in the faces of those who have so much trouble letting the Child within have expression in their lives through playfulness, joy, happiness, and fun—it deeply saddens me. I can hardly comprehend what this must feel like because my Child is such a strong part of me. Give the Child a voice? I think mine speaks up loud and clear. Give her *permission* to come out? Mine has been running the show! I am thirty-seven now, and still feel like a kid in an adult-sized body.

I got the same messages that most everyone else got—to grow up, straighten up, be serious, be responsible—basically to stop having fun. When I was reprimanded, scolded, or lectured by my parents, teachers, or other adults, I never took it in on any deep level. I may have altered my behavior in the moment, but I didn't alter my being. Even as a small child I think I knew that a large part of my reason for being on this planet was to own the joy and happiness and love for life that I came here with, and to live it fully as long as I walk the face of this earth. I knew that I had a treasure, that it was an essential part of me, and that it was important to hang on to it. The negative messages must have rolled off my back. I could see how good it felt to be so joyous and happy, and I could see how much light my little being brought into the lives of others. If they didn't know it was good for them, I sure did!

So that you don't think I've led some sort of charmed life that made it easier for me to stay in touch with my playful Child, let me tell you a bit about myself. I was raised in a small Southern town where manners and "ladylike" behavior were of the utmost importance, and I was told to act or not act a certain way thousands of times, because otherwise, "What will the neighbors think?" Also my household was strict Southern Baptist, so I got messages not only from my mom but from God to walk the straight and narrow path. My adult life hasn't been such a breeze either. I was married at twenty-four, and a year later my husband was killed in a plane crash when I was eight and a half months pregnant. My second marriage seven years later has involved dealing with my husband's drug addiction. It's been a long, hard road going through the ordeal of the drugs, the lying, and finally the recovery. But through it all my spirit has never broken. On the contrary, my happy, loving outlook on life is what saw me through the troubled times. The ability to find the brighter side of things, to embrace the happy moments while healing the pain—these were choices that enabled me to hold on to the loving Child in my heart.

So what does being playful mean? Playfulness doesn't require a special setting or a bag of tricks. It means being spontaneous, seizing every opportunity to be playful *in the moment*. The foremost question in a child's mind is probably, "Will it be fun?" I think it's important for us to ask that question of ourselves as adults. I know for me that if it's not fun, it usually doesn't make it into my list of things to do. And if you're a little creative, you can turn even the most mundane chores into fun. Ever give your grocery cart a big push and ride it to your car?

Thinking and writing about playfulness has made me realize what an enormous impact it has had on who I am in the world, and how much it has empowered me as a person. My childlike quality has certainly made me less defensive, more open, more curious, more eager to grow—just like a child. I look for delight and wonder in the world around me, and you know, there's so much there, when we just look. I see that my playfulness invites others to be playful, that people are drawn to me for that reason, and that my happiness has healed a lot of hearts. I believe that loving little Child is in all of us.

And to top it off, even my *work* is fun. I have always worked in the field of art, but only in the past four or five years have I found my true expression, and I am very successful at it. I create one-of-a-kind pieces of art to wear from head to toe, and I have free creative rein in what I do. My clients usually tell me only to let my imagination go further than it did on the last piece. My work is not only enhanced, it *depends* on my staying in touch with the fun-loving part of myself, with my sensual Child, my Child that's uninhibited and free to create from her heart's center.

I must admit that at one time my being so childlike seemed to have a small disadvantage: I was afraid to own my power as a woman, because I thought that being powerful meant I'd have to give up my playfulness. The adults in my life when I was young were, with a few notable exceptions, serious, proper, and stuffy. And I decided I never wanted to be like that! So for me, it was an either/or situation, and I opted for the playful Child. So as an adult I sometimes behaved like a shy little girl, afraid to be assertive, even equipped with a little-girl voice. It wasn't until Margie pointed this out to me one day that I became aware of it, and I noticed that I had *new* role models around me now, people like Margie and Erika, who were in touch with their playfulness but also owned their power as women in the world. What a revelation this was to me—that I could continue to dress the way I wanted to, act crazy or silly if I wanted to, and also come into my power as a woman. Being conscious of this awareness has made a real difference in my life. I feel like a whole person now—still like a kid in an adult-sized body—but with the power to create what I want in my life, the power to be all that I can be.

When we are truly connected to our Inner Child, we express a sense of inner power and control over our own lives and are not easily controlled by others. Because parents and society have always been threatened by a loss of control, we all received many erroneous messages about who the Child really is. As adults we generally harbor many false beliefs about the Inner Child. Some of the more common erroneous beliefs are:

- The Inner Child doesn't exist in me; maybe in others, but not in me.
- Everyone will think I'm too optimistic and not take me seriously.
- No one will see my depth if I'm *that* happy.
- Everyone else will just bring me down again.

- Being connected to the Inner Child is not a choice I can make, it just happens when things go right.
- No one at work—my boss, fellow employees, students, clients— would respect me if I were childlike.
- People will just say I'm irresponsible.
- My kids will think I'm just trying to act young; they'll lose respect for me and run all over me.
- Other people will be embarrassed by my spontaneity, and it will be my fault that they are uncomfortable.
- Playing is for kids.
- Others will think I'm a jerk, and I can't handle the disapproval.
- I'll never get anything done if I let the Child in me out.
- I can't trust the Child. It will always get me into trouble.
- If I open to my Child, I will lose control over my life. My Child just wants to control me and everything else.

These are just a few of the false beliefs. There are many others, including the false belief that the Inner Child is incompetent. Nothing could be further from the truth! There is deep wisdom in the Inner Child. This awareness was illustrated to us by Hal, one of our clients.

Hal used to play the piano as a child; as an adult he had wanted to buy one for a long time. The day the piano was delivered he quickly ushered the movers out the door so he could play it right away. Armed with his only piece of sheet music, a Mozart sonata, he attacked the piano. He found that his hands were stiff and the piece was difficult to play. But Hal was going to make this fun no matter how hard it was, or what it took to finish the piece. Within a few moments his body was rigid and sweating. His face was tense and frowning, but at last he was the conqueror—he finished it! A little voice within him asked, "Yes, but was it fun?" and he suddenly remembered why he gave up the piano in the first place! Feeling totally bewildered, he decided to throw the music away and just play what he felt. In that moment he set his Inner Child free and what flowed from the golden strings of the piano was the sound of joy and creativity that he had so long denied. What he learned was that trying to "do it right" was hardly fulfilling. His Inner Child knew how to play all along, and the sound was magnificent.

So you may be saying, "Of course he could do that. He already knew how to play as a child, so that's how he would remember it. But you can't trust the Child to just take over any activity, especially one

that could be dangerous. The Child cannot be trusted to learn important things—it just doesn't have the understanding." Erika had a
remarkable experience, however, in which she learned she could do
just that:

I am a glider pilot and I had wanted to be one ever since I was a little girl and
saw a Disney movie about soaring. For various reasons, I started late in life—
only a few years ago—but that beginning taught me a lesson about my Inner
Child I'll never forget.

It was a warm October day when we drove out to the desert for my first,
very-long-awaited lesson. I had asked a friend to go with me to Crystal Soaring
in the Mojave Desert because I was so excited I could hardly drive.

Sitting in the front seat of that beautiful glider I fell in love with her long
wings. I was as ecstatic as John Stevenson, my flight instructor, and I started
down the runway behind the tow plane. During the whole flight I heard my
voice saying "Wow!" as the dream I had lived for became real. Then John said,
"Erika, take the controls and roll us into a turn." It was enormously empowering to feel the wings respond to me: I felt part of the eagle's domain. It
seemed to me that if I could do this in the air, there wasn't anything that I
couldn't do on the ground. As we landed I felt teary at the overwhelming
beauty and fun that I experienced.

My second lesson was a very different experience, however. As I buckled
my seatbelts I was aware of feeling tense and unsure. A critical voice inside me
said, "Erika, you can't fly and you will make such a bad mistake that John will
never get you out of it. This is not fun, you know, you're taking a serious risk
here and you will probably kill John, too." I felt queasy on the takeoff, and this
time when I took the controls I couldn't hold them tight enough. My arm was
rigid with fear, so I jerked the wings around instead of rolling them smoothly
as I had naturally done the week before. I was terrified, and when we landed
I wasn't sure I would go up again. I kept all of this from John in case he would
not see how serious this was. I was worried he would think I was just being
hysterical, rather than realizing that we were going to die!

As I drove home from that lesson I was more than disappointed, I was
defeated. Later I realized that I had disconnected from my Child in the second
lesson due to my fear; that my Inner Child, connected to my Adult, had flown
the first lesson. I decided I would always let my Child participate in the flying.
That's it!! My Inner Child *knows*!! I had believed that I couldn't trust the knowledge of my Inner Child, and that if I just had fun I would surely die.

In the next lesson, as we rolled down the runway, I started to feel tense
again, so I opened the window and visualized dumping my fear out and then
slammed the window shut! I felt free again, and the wings once again became
the extension of my Child's spirit. My flight training progressed at an unusually
rapid pace as my skills matured very quickly. Part of this was due to John. He
is a perfect balance of Adult and Child. When he teaches, his Adult gives him

superb mastery of the plane. His highly developed Child gives him sensitivity to and intuitive knowledge of the air, the plane, and his pupils.

To this day, whenever I fly, each takeoff reminds me of the value in allowing the Inner Child to soar.

The following chart is a summary of the definition of the loved Inner Child:

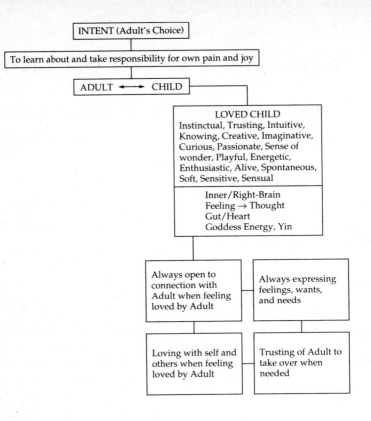

CHAPTER 2

You Are an Adult/Parent

The way we were treated as small children is the way we treat
ourselves the rest of our life.

For Your Own Good
ALICE MILLER

The Adult part of us does not suddenly come into being when we turn
eighteen. From the time we are born we are developing both the Child
and the Adult parts of ourselves.

Defining the Adult

The Adult is the logical, thinking part of us. The feelings of the
Adult come from thought, as opposed to the Child, whose thoughts
come from its feelings. The Adult is concerned with doing rather than
being, with acting rather than experiencing. We can conceive of the
Adult as the yang, the masculine, or the left-brain aspect of ourselves
and the Child as the yin, feminine, or right-brain aspect. We can think
of the Adult as the conscious mind, the linear-thinking intellect.

The Adult is the *choicemaker* regarding intent and actions. *It is always
the Adult that chooses to protect or chooses to learn and chooses the actions that
follow the intent.* It is up to the Adult to initiate the task of loving re-
parenting—of healing the old wounds and replacing false beliefs with
the truth—and to refuse to condone the destructive or self-destructive
patterns of the abandoned Child. The Inner Child will be naturally
curious and open to learning when the Adult has chosen to learn and
to love the Child consistently.

Our Inner Adult may be a loving Adult or an unloving Adult—in
other words, an Adult who has chosen to learn or an Adult who has
chosen to protect. Before we describe these, however, it is important to
have a working definition of loving behavior: *we are being loving when we
choose to nurture and support our own and others' emotional/spiritual growth
and when we take personal responsibility for our feelings—that is, when we*

do not act as victims and do not make others responsible for our actions and reactions and the resulting happiness or unhappiness. In addition, loving behavior is honesty with yourself about yourself and is nonshaming toward yourself and others. It is always inwardly harmonious, thus enhancing your self-esteem and sense of integrity. Loving behavior with your Inner Child means that you take responsibility for your own feelings by learning with your Child about the false beliefs that are causing your pain. It means that you create a loving and supportive arena in which to move through old anger and pain, and that you discover what brings you joy, and act to bring it about.

The Unloving Adult

The unloving Adult is the Adult who has made the choice to protect him/herself against perceiving, experiencing, feeling, and taking responsibility for the pain, fear, sadness, discomfort, and intense aloneness and loneliness of the Inner Child. The unloving Adult also chooses to avoid responsibility for the Child's joy. It puts tasks, rules, obligations, and shaming ahead of connectedness. The unloving Adult thus disconnects from and abandons the Inner Child by being either an authoritarian or permissive Inner Parent. When the unloving Adult is being authoritarian, it is critical, judgmental, shaming, discounting, and/or controlling. It is the inner voice that lies to the Child, telling the Child it is bad, wrong, inadequate, stupid, selfish, or unimportant, and invalidates the Child's feelings. It attempts to control the Child by telling it what it "should" or "should not" do and all the bad things that will happen if it doesn't "do it right." The unloving Adult tells the Child it is loving only if it is self-sacrificing and that it is selfish to make oneself happy, when the truth is that selfishness is expecting others to take responsibility for your feelings. The unloving Adult makes unilateral decisions, discounting the Child's wants and needs. The unloving Adult ignores and negates the voice of the Inner Child, creating the same sorts of difficulties that parents have when they don't listen to their children. The primary intent of the unloving Adult when it is being authoritarian is to maintain control over the Inner Child.

The unloving Adult, having absorbed a set of rules from parents and society, imposes these rules on the Inner Child. Melody Beattie, in *Beyond Codependence*, lists a number of rules that most of us have absorbed:

- Don't feel or talk about feelings.

- Don't think, figure things out, or make decisions—you probably don't know what you want or what's best for you.

- Don't identify, mention, or solve problems—it's not okay to have them.

- Be good, right, perfect, and strong.

- Don't be who you are because that's not good enough.

- Don't be selfish, put yourself first, say what you want and need, say no, set boundaries, or take care of yourself—always take care of others and never hurt their feelings or make them angry.

- Don't have fun, be silly, or enjoy life—it costs money, makes noise, and isn't necessary.

- Don't trust yourself, your Higher Power, the process of life, or certain people—instead put your faith in untrustworthy people; then act surprised when they let you down.

- Don't be open, honest, and direct—hint, manipulate, get others to talk for you, guess what they want and need, and expect them to do the same for you.

- Don't get close to people—it isn't safe.

- Don't disrupt the system by growing or changing.

- Always *look* good, no matter how you feel or what you have to do.

Our unloving Adult may continue to impose these rules and false beliefs on our Inner Child, thus perpetuating the unlovingness we experienced as children.

When the unloving Adult is being permissive, it may be completely absent, leaving the Child to deal with everything alone. Or, it may be neglectful and indulgent, allowing the Child to be self-destructive, to abuse and violate itself, physically and/or emotionally, through substance and process addictions. The indulgent Inner Adult may also allow the Inner Child to be destructive to others through physical and/or emotional violence—hitting, beating, stealing, lying, shaming, or even raping and killing. The permissive unloving Adult may resist the wants and needs of the Inner Child. The unloving Adult has chosen to resist responsibility for meeting the needs of the Inner Child, leaving the Child to get its needs met through others.

Both the authoritarian and permissive Inner Adult leave the Inner Child feeling unloved and abandoned. The Child concludes that it is bad, wrong, unlovable, defective, unimportant, insignificant, and inadequate, and these false beliefs create feelings of fear, shame, and guilt.

The unloving Adult is generally a carbon copy of the unlovingness of our parents, grandparents, siblings, teachers, clergy, or other role models and authority figures. We all have a tendency to respond to our Inner Child in much the same way our parents or caretakers responded to us, thereby perpetuating our pain and sense of disconnection. We may criticize, lie, shame, and discount our Inner Child in much the same way we were criticized, lied to, shamed, and discounted as children, often using the same words, phrases, and actions. Your unloving Adult will be authoritarian or permissive, depending on how your parents or other primary caretakers treated you and themselves.

Your inner dialogue, which takes place all the time unconsciously, is probably similar to the words you heard as a child from your role models. Our parents most likely parented us from their abandoned Child and unloving Adult, which became the role model for our own unloving Adult.

If you were unlovingly parented as a child—and almost all of us were to varying degrees—you may have absorbed the same false beliefs under which your parents' abandoned Inner Child operated. Below are a few of the false beliefs that you may have absorbed from watching and experiencing your parents:

- I can't make myself happy; I can't make myself as happy as someone or something else can; I can't take care of myself.

- I can't handle pain, especially the pain of rejection and abandonment, the pain of my aloneness.

- Others are responsible for my feelings and I'm responsible for theirs.

- I can control how others feel about me and treat me.

- Resisting control is essential to my integrity.

- Making myself happy is selfish and therefore wrong.

- My core self is bad, wrong, unlovable, or in some way defective.

There is a good possibility that as long as you operate from these false beliefs you will not move into loving behavior with your Inner Child. You will not take responsibility for your own feelings and choose to learn if you believe you are bad and incapable of making yourself happy and that you cannot handle your Inner Child's pain. You will instead continue to attempt to control your Inner Child, who will in turn try to control others. You will continue to make others responsible for your feelings by abandoning your Inner Child. Once your Adult has chosen to abandon your Inner Child, your Child is left powerless and alone. It is the Adult that must initially make a new choice on the Child's behalf.

The chart on p. 24 illustrates the unloving Adult.

The Loving Adult

The loving Adult—the Adult who has chosen to learn from and with the Inner Child—is the powerful, committed, courageous aspect of ourselves, the part of ourselves that is ethical and acts with integrity. The loving Adult is deeply *committed* to learning how to re-parent the Inner Child. It is deeply committed to knowing, loving, nurturing, supporting, and connecting with the Inner Child. Within the loving Adult lies the *courage* to look within, to face ourselves, and know ourselves. This is the positive Inner Parent, the part of ourselves that can heal old wounds from childhood and replace false beliefs with the truth. This is the aspect of ourselves that can act in a positive way in behalf of the feelings and needs of the Inner Child. It can bring to fruition through action the wants, needs, desires, and creative ideas of the Child. The Child is hungry, so the Adult prepares food. The Child is tired, so the Adult gets in bed and turns out the light. The Child wants to connect with others, so the Adult makes the phone call. The Child creates the image and the Adult translates it onto canvas.

The Adult expresses through action the needs and feelings of both the Child and the Adult. Experiencing feelings without the action of the Adult leaves us stuck. Likewise, action without feeling behind it is an empty experience. For example, if you feel warmth toward someone, but do not express it with some form of action, they never get a true experience of you. However, if you act affectionate without a feeling of love, then the act is empty, and may even be manipulative. This is why the connection and balance between the two is so important. When the loving Adult and the loved Child work together, there is harmony within.

The loving Adult is neither authoritarian nor permissive with the Inner Child. The Adult does not impose its will on the Child and force the Child to do things its way, nor is the loving Adult indulgent towards the Child. The Inner Child may want to eat candy all day, but the loving Adult does not act on this. Instead, the loving Adult asks the Child why it wants this, why is it feeling so empty that it needs to fill up with candy? The loving Adult does not shame the Child for what it

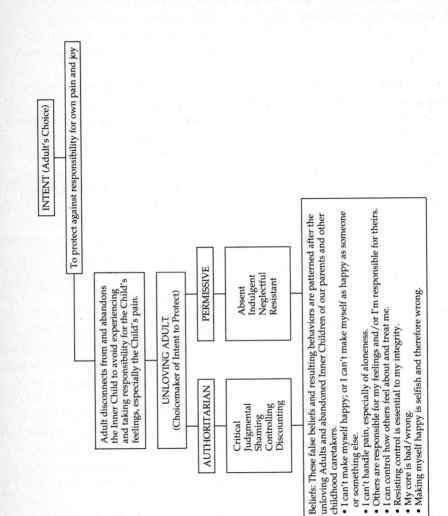

INTENT (Adult's Choice)

To protect against responsibility for own pain and joy

Adult disconnects from and abandons the Inner Child to avoid experiencing and taking responsibility for the Child's feelings, especially the Child's pain.

UNLOVING ADULT
(Choicemaker of Intent to Protect)

AUTHORITARIAN

Critical
Judgmental
Shaming
Controlling
Discounting

PERMISSIVE

Absent
Indulgent
Neglectful
Resistant

Beliefs: These false beliefs and resulting behaviors are patterned after the unloving Adults and abandoned Inner Children of our parents and other childhood caretakers.
• I can't make myself happy; or I can't make myself as happy as someone or something else.
• I can't handle pain, especially of aloneness.
• Others are responsible for my feelings and/or I'm responsible for theirs.
• I can control how others feel about and treat me.
• Resisting control is essential to my integrity.
• My core is bad/wrong.
• Making myself happy is selfish and therefore wrong.

wants and feels, does not tell the Child it is wrong or bad. The Adult knows that the Child has important reasons for feeling as it does and acts with the intent to learn about these feelings.

The loving Adult does not indulge the Child in allowing unloving behavior towards others. The Inner Child may feel enraged at another person. The loving Adult is open to learning about and understanding this rage and helps the Child express it in appropriate ways, but does not allow the Child to dump its rage on others in ways that are manipulative or harmful—to bully, threaten, or physically harm others. The loving Adult does not abandon the Child when the Child is angry, hurt, or sad, nor does it tell the Child that others are responsible for these feelings. The Adult knows that these feelings come from within, from the internal fears and beliefs, rather than being *caused* by someone else and is there to hear and understand the Child's feelings and help the Child to heal. In addition, the Adult protects the Child from taking things personally by always telling the Child the truth. For example, let's say that your spouse yells at you and tells you you're stupid. As a child you may have been told that time and time again by your parents, and so you are sensitive to being called stupid. A loving Adult would step in and say to the Child, "That angry and judgmental behavior has nothing to do with you. You are an intelligent person. That put-down comes from something that is going on with him/her, for which you are not responsible. So don't worry, I'll handle this situation for us." The Adult then acts in the Child's behalf and says to your spouse, "I know you're upset, but I don't want to be put down. This doesn't feel good. When you're open, then let's talk." Then the Adult would leave the scene if he/she is not open to learning. If the Child is still feeling hurt from the insult, the Adult would listen to the Child's feelings and attempt to learn more about the source of these feelings, perhaps remembering long-buried childhood memories of similar situations. The Adult trusts that the Child's feelings are not arbitrary, that they come from the Child's past experiences and from the beliefs that resulted from these experiences. The loving Adult is a teacher and heals the Child's false belief system by telling the Child the truth.

The loving Adult is personally powerful, in the sense of having power over self, choice, and the ability to realize dreams, the dreams of the Child. The chart on p. 26 illustrates the characteristics of the loving Adult and the loved Child and the connection between the two.

Becoming aware of the unloving way in which we are parenting ourselves and what it means to be a loving Adult to our Inner Child is the most important thing we can each do for ourselves. The way we each treat our Inner Child

Inner Adult Connecting to Inner Child

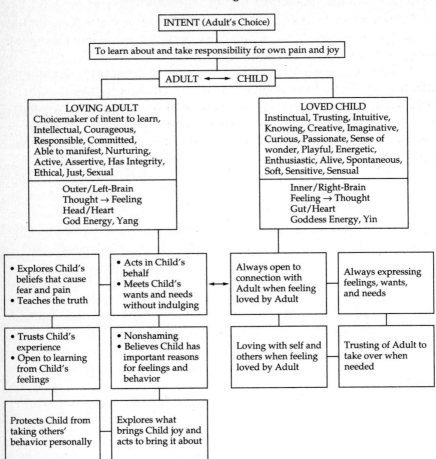

INTENT (Adult's Choice)

To learn about and take responsibility for own pain and joy

ADULT ←→ CHILD

LOVING ADULT
Choicemaker of intent to learn,
Intellectual, Courageous,
Responsible, Committed,
Able to manifest, Nurturing,
Active, Assertive, Has Integrity,
Ethical, Just, Sexual

Outer/Left-Brain
Thought → Feeling
Head/Heart
God Energy, Yang

LOVED CHILD
Instinctual, Trusting, Intuitive,
Knowing, Creative, Imaginative,
Curious, Passionate, Sense of
wonder, Playful, Energetic,
Enthusiastic, Alive, Spontaneous,
Soft, Sensitive, Sensual

Inner/Right-Brain
Feeling → Thought
Gut/Heart
Goddess Energy, Yin

- Explores Child's
  beliefs that cause
  fear and pain
- Teaches the truth

- Acts in Child's
  behalf
- Meets Child's
  wants and needs
  without indulging

Always open to
connection with
Adult when feeling
loved by Adult

Always expressing
feelings, wants,
and needs

- Trusts Child's
  experience
- Open to learning
  from Child's
  feelings

- Nonshaming
- Believes Child has
  important reasons
  for feelings and
  behavior

Loving with self and
others when feeling
loved by Adult

Trusting of Adult to
take over when
needed

Protects Child from
taking others'
behavior personally

Explores what
brings Child joy and
acts to bring it about

causes everything else in our lives. Treating our Inner Child unlovingly results in substance and process addictions, and creates fear, anxiety, depression, pain, emptiness, neediness, low self-esteem, and an unbearable sense of aloneness, as well as physical and mental illness. The severity of mental illness from which a person suffers is directly related to the degree of internal disconnection between the Inner Adult and the Inner Child. Craziness results when we avoid facing and feeling the deep aloneness and pain of the Inner Child.

Treating our Inner Child lovingly creates the inner connection that fills the emptiness from within rather than needing to fill it externally with addictions. The more we learn to treat our Inner Child lovingly, the more solid and full the internal connection becomes, leading to peace, joy, power, and wholeness, erasing the need to give ourselves up to be loved by others.

CHAPTER 3

The Ego and the Higher Self

*Truth does not fight against illusions, nor do illusions fight against
the truth. Illusions battle only with themselves.*
                                                    A Course in Miracles

All the problems in our society stem from the internal disconnection
between the Adult and the Child. All unloving acts toward others and
toward the planet are manifestations of the internal disconnection and
abandonment, which is handed down from one generation to the next.
Once the Adult disconnects from the Child and is unavailable to act in
behalf of the Inner Child's softness, lovingness, and sense of unity with
others, then the unloving Adult and the abandoned Child wreak havoc
within themselves and with others, particularly within families. The
fear created through the internal abandonment is projected onto others
and acted out through violence and war. We will not be capable of fully
solving the problems of child abuse, crime, war, hunger, and pollution
of the planet until enough people do their inner work and learn to
function from their Higher Selves.

The Higher Self

Dr. Charles Whitfield, in *Healing the Child Within*, defines the Child
as "our Real Self—who we truly are." He states that "In this book I use
the following terms interchangeably: Real Self, True Self, Child Within,
Inner Child, Divine Child, and Higher Self." Philip Oliver-Diaz and
Patricia A. O'Gorman, in *12 Steps to Self-Parenting*, state that the Higher
Parent (what we are calling the loving Adult) "is the transcendent part
of yourself, a direct channel to your Higher Power." They go on to state
that ". . . the presence of the divinity within, the Higher Parent in each
of us is what has sustained us."

It seems that one author states that the Child is the Higher Self and
the other states that the loving Adult is the Higher Self. We have a
third opinion. We believe that it is the *connection between the loving Adult*

and the loved Inner Child that is the Higher Self. The connection and balance between the two—the Adult/Child, the God/Goddess, the masculine/feminine, the yin/yang—constitute the Higher Self.

We define the Higher Self as our wholeness, ability to love, and sense of personal power—who we truly are, our true identity. It is who we are when we are connected to the universe, and we believe this universal connection occurs when we establish the inner connection between the Adult and the Child. The Higher Self is who we are when we are most authentic, genuine, and compassionate. When we are in the connected state of the Higher Self, we are filled with love, empathy, and forgiveness. It is the wondrous state that enables us to draw upon our wisdom, the wisdom that comes directly from the universe.

The Higher Self is the essence of power, the generative, nurturing, life-giving, and life-sustaining creative element within ourselves and in the universe. It is from the balance between the God and the Goddess, the masculine and the feminine that all life springs forth. It is nonviolent, it never takes life, it never destroys; it only gives life and love, and is, therefore, the essence of peace.

The Higher Self state is the powerful healing state of the shamans. Shamans tap into what some call their "feminine" side, what we are referring to as the Child, in order to heal. In *Healing States*, the authors Alberto Villoldo and Stanley Krippner talked to a renowned South American shaman about this concept: "When we asked don Eduardo what he meant by learning to 'see,' he replied that a shaman was not able to 'see' with his or her inner vision until his or her feminine side was awakened. Our masculine, rational side, he claimed, allowed us to see only the surface of things." It is through the Adult/Child, masculine/feminine connection that the shaman is able to see and know in an inner way and thereby heal. When a person is open to learning and healing, the power, wisdom, and tenderness of the Higher Self can heal any hurt, comfort any pain, and deplete any anger. It is the Higher Self that most activates the immune system, creating excellent physical health.

Whenever we experience an expansive feeling of love and unity with all of humanity, it is because we are deeply connected within; we are our Higher Selves. The chart on p.30 illustrates how the Higher Self evolves through the connection between the Adult and Child.

The purpose of the Higher Self is to learn and love and grow into total joy. Think of a memory in which you feel totally peaceful, or wildly in love, or in which you experience deep joy, or an exhilarating sense of inner strength and personal power. The feeling you get from

Inner Adult Connecting to Inner Child

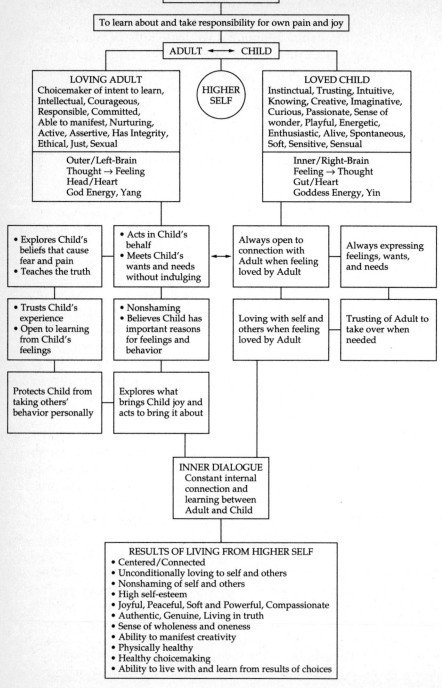

INTENT (Adult's Choice)

To learn about and take responsibility for own pain and joy

ADULT ⟷ CHILD

LOVING ADULT
Choicemaker of intent to learn, Intellectual, Courageous, Responsible, Committed, Able to manifest, Nurturing, Active, Assertive, Has Integrity, Ethical, Just, Sexual

Outer/Left-Brain
Thought → Feeling
Head/Heart
God Energy, Yang

HIGHER SELF

LOVED CHILD
Instinctual, Trusting, Intuitive, Knowing, Creative, Imaginative, Curious, Passionate, Sense of wonder, Playful, Energetic, Enthusiastic, Alive, Spontaneous, Soft, Sensitive, Sensual

Inner/Right-Brain
Feeling → Thought
Gut/Heart
Goddess Energy, Yin

- Explores Child's beliefs that cause fear and pain
- Teaches the truth

- Acts in Child's behalf
- Meets Child's wants and needs without indulging

Always open to connection with Adult when feeling loved by Adult

Always expressing feelings, wants, and needs

- Trusts Child's experience
- Open to learning from Child's feelings

- Nonshaming
- Believes Child has important reasons for feelings and behavior

Loving with self and others when feeling loved by Adult

Trusting of Adult to take over when needed

Protects Child from taking others' behavior personally

Explores what brings Child joy and acts to bring it about

INNER DIALOGUE
Constant internal connection and learning between Adult and Child

RESULTS OF LIVING FROM HIGHER SELF
- Centered/Connected
- Unconditionally loving to self and others
- Nonshaming of self and others
- High self-esteem
- Joyful, Peaceful, Soft and Powerful, Compassionate
- Authentic, Genuine, Living in truth
- Sense of wholeness and oneness
- Ability to manifest creativity
- Physically healthy
- Healthy choicemaking
- Ability to live with and learn from results of choices

that memory is your Higher Self. It is a sense of inner peace, uncon-ditional love, and awareness. The Higher Self does not judge, fear, worry, or deny; it is totally "in the moment." Though most of us can recall this feeling at one time or another, we seldom think of living our day-to-day lives in such a wonderful state. All of us can choose to be our Higher Selves any time we choose to connect lovingly with our Inner Child. But most of us have spent so much time being discon-nected that we no longer know how to connect with ourselves. Some of us may never have known how in this life. It is the internal disconnection between the Adult and the Child that creates the ego.

The Ego

Our use of the term *ego* needs some clarification. We do not mean ego in the sense of Freud's ego or ego psychology. Our definition of the ego comes more from Eastern philosophy. We use ego to mean the false self that emerges whenever we choose to protect instead of to learn. When we responded to the external rejection we experienced as children by internally rejecting ourselves, we disconnected and the ego emerged. While most of us disconnected and abandoned ourselves to one degree or another, there are those few children who never did abandon themselves. A good example of this is illustrated in the won-derful little book, *Mr. God, This is Anna*, by Fynn, a true story about a little girl who ran away from abusive parents and found loving people to take care of her. Anna, a beautiful example of a connected human being, became Fynn's teacher at the age of five.

Early in your life, when you were very small, you experienced your first separation, your first disconnection from a primary person in your life. In our society this generally happens at birth when the infant is taken away from the mother and put into a nursery, left to face this world alone. When you arrived home, instead of being held in arms and made to feel loved and safe, you were often left in your crib or playpen alone. (We recommend reading *The Continuum Concept* by Jean Liedloff for a description of a society that functions very differently from ours.) Then other rejections and disconnections followed. It may have been something small like a late feeding, or something large like the death of a parent. It may have been that you didn't get the love, affirmation, and acceptance that you needed from your mother or fa-ther. Perhaps you experienced overt or covert disapproval for being yourself. We all experienced many forms of disconnection from our parents, and we each concluded that we were being rejected or abandoned because there was something wrong with us—we were inadequate or bad and unlovable. At that moment the ego was born. In that tiny, vulnerable time, what we experienced as rejection and the resulting experience of aloneness was too much to handle, so we attempted to protect ourselves by disconnecting from the Child that felt so alone, and constructed a false self—the ego—in the hope that it would protect us from the pain of loneliness and get us the love we so desperately needed. As we grew, the external abandonment became more and more internalized, as the ego became stronger and the disconnection between our Inner Adult and our Inner Child became more pronounced.

The purpose of the ego is to protect ourselves against aloneness and to get love, rather than to give love. The ego does not know how to be loving. It is the part of us that is critical, blaming, shaming, frightened, angry, and defensive. The ego manifests itself as the unloving Adult and the unloved abandoned Child. Think of the ego as a troubled person who sits on your shoulder and constantly whispers in your ear, "You can't do it!" "You should have . . ." "No one really loves you," "They don't care about you," "You'll never do it right." These are the distortions of the unloving critical Adult, attempting to get you to change so you will get love and not feel so alone. Or your thoughts might be, "I'll get even with him," "I'll show her she can't do this to me," "No one can tell me what to do." These are the responses of the abandoned Child, attempting to handle the aloneness.

The ego often criticizes the awareness of the Higher Self. One of our clients had an extraordinary experience one evening. She was having company for dinner. They were all in the living room when suddenly she felt a presence tap her on the shoulder and tell her to look at the table. She went to look and saw that the tablecloth had just caught on fire from a fallen candle. No one else had smelled or sensed the fire. The next day her ego discounted the incident, telling her it was just a coincidence.

The ego's job is to fix you or fix others in the hopes of avoiding abandonment and rejection. But paradoxically it is the internal disconnection that creates the ego and brings about the inner experience of separation, abandonment, rejection, and aloneness. It is this disconnection that creates the stress so many of us live with every day. It is this stress that lowers the immune system and thereby leaves the body vulnerable to illness.

The body and the ego go hand in hand. They are related because they are both transitory. The ego thinks the body is the only reality.

The ego does not believe that we are the spiritual love energy of our Higher Selves. Since the ego believes that our physical form is who we are, then if this form isn't "right," we aren't "right," and if this form no longer exists, then we no longer exist. It is because the body and the ego are so closely allied that we have illness, for illness is the body's reflection of the ego's beliefs. Very often the ego attempts to maintain its control over us by giving us false beliefs about our bodies. Much of our low self-esteem comes from the self-limiting ego beliefs we have about our bodies.

The chart on pages 34 and 35, which puts together all we've been saying about the unloving Adult and the unloved Child, illustrates how the ego is created through the disconnection that occurs from the intent to protect against being personally responsible for our feelings of pain, fear, discomfort, peace, and joy.

Beliefs Versus Truth

Any belief that causes us anxiety, hurt, or fear is a false belief, and anytime we are anxious or hurt, we are operating from a false belief. Our sadness and grief come from seeing and experiencing the truth about a situation, but our hurt, anxiety, and fear come from our false beliefs. As children, most of us adopted beliefs that aren't true for us, and so they cause us pain. We may have absorbed beliefs like "I'm not pretty," or "I'm stupid," or "No one can love me the way I am," and these beliefs hurt us. *If a belief causes us pain, then it is a false belief.* If what you believe to be true hurts you, then believing it does not work for you, and it is important to recognize that it is an ego belief and therefore erroneous, since all of the ego's beliefs are erroneous. The Higher Self does not have beliefs, it is only aware of the truth, and so what we know from our Higher Self never causes us to hurt. Part of the growth process involves identifying our ego beliefs and correcting the ones that cause us pain.

We established the beliefs that make up our egos when we were very small, sometimes even at birth. Pat, a woman in one of our workshops, remembered an ego belief that she established at birth and that has affected her whole life.

I've always been so afraid of others' disapproval. I've actually believed I had to be perfect or I would be *killed*. It never made any sense to me until now. What I just remembered was that I was a twin when I was born. My twin sister was born deformed and she died. But I didn't know that she died by herself.

Inner Adult Disconnecting from Inner Child

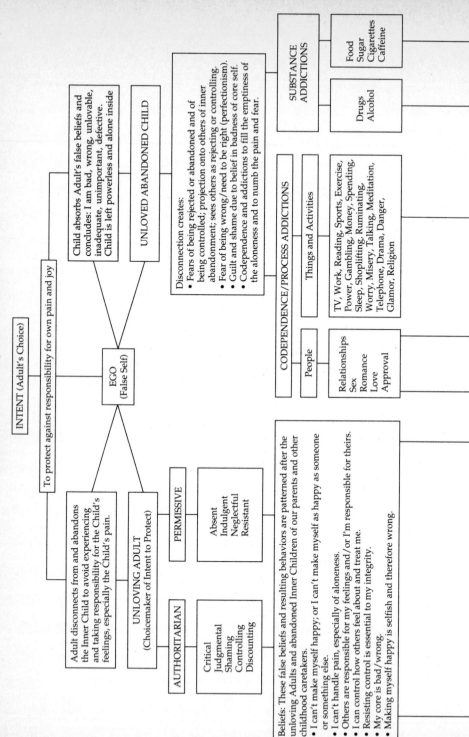

INTENT (Adult's Choice)

To protect against responsibility for own pain and joy

EGO (False Self)

Adult disconnects from and abandons the Inner Child to avoid experiencing and taking responsibility for the Child's feelings, especially the Child's pain.

Child absorbs Adult's false beliefs and concludes: I am bad, wrong, unlovable, inadequate, unimportant, defective. Child is left powerless and alone inside

UNLOVED ABANDONED CHILD

Disconnection creates:
- Fears of being rejected or abandoned and of being controlled; projection onto others of inner abandonment; sees others as rejecting or controlling.
- Fear of being wrong/need to be right (perfectionism).
- Guilt and shame due to belief in badness of core self.
- Codependence and addictions to fill the emptiness of the aloneness and to numb the pain and fear.

UNLOVING ADULT (Choicemaker of Intent to Protect)

AUTHORITARIAN

Critical
Judgmental
Shaming
Controlling
Discounting

PERMISSIVE

Absent
Indulgent
Neglectful
Resistant

Beliefs: These false beliefs and resulting behaviors are patterned after the unloving Adults and abandoned Inner Children of our parents and other childhood caretakers.
- I can't make myself happy; or I can't make myself as happy as someone or something else.
- I can't handle pain, especially of aloneness.
- Others are responsible for my feelings and/or I'm responsible for theirs.
- I can control how others feel about and treat me.
- Resisting control is essential to my integrity.
- My core is bad/wrong.
- Making myself happy is selfish and therefore wrong.

CODEPENDENCE/PROCESS ADDICTIONS

People

Relationships
Sex
Romance
Love
Approval

Things and Activities

TV, Work, Reading, Sports, Exercise, Power, Gambling, Money, Spending, Sleep, Shoplifting, Ruminating, Worry, Misery, Talking, Meditation, Telephone, Drama, Danger, Glamor, Religion

SUBSTANCE ADDICTIONS

Drugs
Alcohol

Food
Sugar
Cigarettes
Caffeine

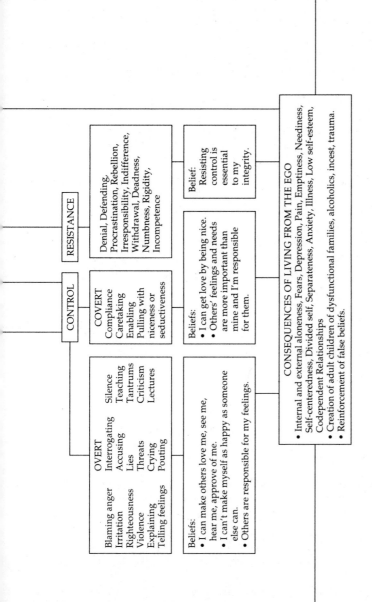

CONTROL

OVERT

Interrogating
Accusing
Lies
Threats
Crying
Pouting

Silence
Teaching
Tantrums
Criticism
Lectures

Blaming anger
Irritation
Righteousness
Violence
Explaining
Telling feelings

Beliefs:
• I can make others love me, see me, hear me, approve of me.
• I can't make myself as happy as someone else can.
• Others are responsible for my feelings.

COVERT

Compliance
Caretaking
Enabling
Pulling with niceness or seductiveness

Beliefs:
• I can get love by being nice.
• Others' feelings and needs are more important than mine and I'm responsible for them.

RESISTANCE

Denial, Defending, Procrastination, Rebellion, Irresponsibility, Indifference, Withdrawal, Deadness, Numbness, Rigidity, Incompetence

Belief: Resisting control is essential to my integrity.

CONSEQUENCES OF LIVING FROM THE EGO
• Internal and external aloneness, Fears, Depression, Pain, Emptiness, Neediness, Self-centeredness, Divided self, Separateness, Anxiety, Illness, Low self-esteem, Codependent Relationships
• Creation of adult children of dysfunctional families, alcoholics, incest, trauma.
• Reinforcement of false beliefs.

I thought my parents killed her because she wasn't perfect. So I've carried around the belief that my parents or other people would kill me if I wasn't perfect.

We establish our erroneous, self-limiting beliefs in an attempt to protect ourselves from rejection, abandonment, or even death. Margie recalls how this happened for her.

In a rebirthing session (a form of body therapy that helps you remember your birth) I clearly remembered my birth. I saw my mother lying there so drugged that she was actually out of her body. The only other person in the room was the doctor (this was in a small town). He was an uncaring, detached man, anxious to get the birth over with. (I later was able to confirm this with my mother. I was even able to describe exactly how the doctor looked, how the labor table was facing, and the color of the walls of the delivery room.) I remembered coming into the world and feeling so very alone, so disconnected from anyone. It felt as if my heart would break from feeling so alone, and at that moment I established one of my core ego beliefs—*I'm not important.* I concluded that I wasn't important because nobody was there to greet me and the doctor was irritated with me.

The next memory was of the nursery. I was the only baby there, and a couple of nurses were fussing over me. I heard one of them say, "She's such a good baby, she never cries." From that I concluded that the way to get love and attention was to be "good." Being good meant never complaining and going along with whatever someone wanted of me. I kept this belief for many years and it caused me much pain. It led to my being compliant and not taking responsibility for my own wants and desires, as well as becoming a caretaker for others. It has taken me many years to give up this erroneous, limiting ego belief.

As infants and small children we are primarily concerned with getting love, since without it we could die. To really grow up means to move from always needing to get love into giving love to ourselves and others, which happens only when we finally stop running from our pain and shame and when we successfully heal the grief from past experiences of loss, trauma, or abuse. Only then can we explore and discard the limiting beliefs from the ego and open ourselves to the truth of the Higher Self. Below is an example from Erika's experience of how as a child she adopted a self-limiting belief.

They say that as children we adopt our favorite story and somehow make it part of our life script. My favorite story was *The Wizard of Oz.* My favorite line in the movie was when the Wizard gives the Tin Man his heart and says: "and remember, my friend, that the heart is not judged by how much you love, but by how much you are loved by others." These words spoken by the Wizard himself had to be true, and I believed him with all my heart. The only problem is, it's backwards. The heart can only be judged as loving if it *is* loving! The saying should go: "the heart is not judged by how much you are loved by others, but by how much you love." As a consequence I spent most of my childhood concerned with how many people loved me rather than learning to be the most loving person I could be. If someone rejected me, it meant my heart was bad and that I was not lovable. I had given the well-being of my self-esteem away to other people, along with my power to know who I was. I always felt scared and unsure as a result. I adopted the beliefs of everyone around me and as a result didn't really know who I was, but I was in pain and hurt most of the time. Seeking the truth about me and about love has freed me from the shackles of the Wizard's belief.

The false beliefs of the ego keep us limited and in pain most of our lives. Below is a list of painful feelings that result from the false beliefs of the ego. These feelings are experienced by both the unloved Inner Child and the unloving Inner Adult.

Ego Feelings

Alone	Confused	Fearful	Hopeless	Powerless	Sickly
Ambivalent	Dead	Fragile	Hurt/In pain	Rageful	Sinful
Angry	Defensive	Frustrated	Incompetent	Regretful	Stupid
Anxious	In denial	Greedy	Indifferent	Resentful	Unworthy
Bad	Depressed	Gulity	Jealous	Righteous	Unlovable
Blaming	Despairing	Hateful	Judgmental	Self-doubting	Vengeful
Bored	Envious	Helpless	Lonely	Shame	Wrong

Out of these feelings come all of our many addictions, which create more painful feelings, locking us into a vicious circle of pain that results from our addictions, and then leads us to seek further addictions to relieve the pain. The ego convinces us that the drug, the food, the alcohol, the approval, the relationship, the TV, the work, sleep, sex, or even anger or depression will relieve the pain, so we become addicted to them, not realizing that they are actually perpetuating the pain.

The ego is based on the false belief that the Inner Child is bad, wrong, unlovable, basically defective, insignificant, unimportant, and/or inadequate. From this core shame-based false belief come all of the other false beliefs of the ego. Below are listed some of the common false beliefs of the ego as manifested through the unloving Adult and the unloved Child:

1. I cannot make myself happy from within myself. Other people, activities, and substances are responsible for making me happy

or unhappy. I am powerless over how I feel and what happens to me. I am a victim.

2. Others' feelings are more important than mine, and I'm responsible for others' feelings. When others feel hurt, disappointed, or upset because of something I've done (with no intent to hurt), I'm wrong and it's my fault. I deserve the guilt I feel. I am selfish if I'm not self-sacrificing.

3. I can't handle pain. The pain will be unending. I will die or go crazy if I'm in pain. To feel pain is to be weak.

4. I can control what others think of me, feel about me, and how they treat me. I can "make" them like me or love me or accept me by being good or nice, and I can "make" them treat me how I want to be treated by getting angry, righteous, and critical when they don't.

5. Resisting others' control is more important than anything. I can preserve my freedom, integrity, and self-esteem by resisting others' control.

6. Taking care of myself and making myself happy is selfish and self-centered, and therefore wrong. A loving person takes care of others' needs and puts one's own aside.

7. Approval = love.

The Higher Self, as manifested through the connection between the loving Adult and the loved Child, knows and tells the truth. Thus the loving Adult tells the Inner Child that it is good, loving, valuable, important, and trustworthy. The loving Adult tells the truth to the Child about the above false beliefs:

1. I have choice over my responses to any situation, and my own choices and responses create my happiness or unhappiness, not other people, activities, or substances.

2. Other people's feelings are the consequences of their own choices regarding their intent, beliefs, and behavior. Therefore, I am not responsible for their feelings, other than if my intent is to hurt. Selfishness is expecting others to be responsible for my feelings. Taking responsibility for my own feelings is loving, not selfish.

3. Pain is a teacher from which I may learn. Pain does not destroy, it only hurts, and I can handle it. Handling pain so that I learn from it is how I get stronger.

4. I have control only over my own beliefs, feelings, and actions, not over anyone else's. I have control only over my own intent, not over anyone else's.

5. Resisting others' control keeps me controlled by my own resistance. It is only when I make my own choices rather than resisting others' choices that I am free.

6. I am being self-responsible when I take care of getting my own needs met and making myself happy. I am being selfish, self-centered, and needy only when I expect others to put themselves aside to meet my needs.

7. Truth = love. When we just offer approval to others, we foster their addiction to our approval. When we tell the truth about ourselves, nonjudgmentally and with compassion, to ourselves and others, we offer them and ourselves a chance to grow.

It is the job of the loving Adult to tell the truth to your ego, as well as to learn why you believe and feel as you do. This is how we are healed from our false beliefs and from the pain of our past. When the loving Adult demonstrates his/her love by telling the truth, then the ego, as manifested by the unloving Adult and the unloved Child, is gradually transformed into the Higher Self.

Since total internal connection is enlightenment, and we personally do not know anyone who has achieved enlightenment, the voice of the ego may always be with us, but we have the choice to be controlled by it or to move into the intent to learn. This becomes easier when we realize that the ego always lies. It thinks and feels in a distorted way, and the truth is, we no longer need to be ruled by its beliefs; but being human, our task is to deal with it. However, the last thing the ego wants is for us to grow and become internally connected, because it fears its own loss of control or death. So as we start to grow, to lovingly connect with the Child within, the ego exerts even more power, throwing more lies at us, telling us that if we continue to reach for our freedom and connection with our Inner Child, we will surely get ourselves into deep trouble or die or end up alone. However, as we become more aware of the loving and nurturing power of the loving Adult, we can use this power within ourselves to transform the fears of the ego into the truth, the love that is within us. We can learn to rely on the loving Adult within us to lovingly re-parent the unloved Inner Child, thereby healing the pain and fear of the ego.

CHAPTER 4

Codependence: A Major Consequence of Disconnection

[Codependence] develops from turning our responsibility for our life and happiness over to our ego and to other people.

Healing the Child Within
CHARLES L. WHITFIELD, M.D.

The paradox that occurs when our Inner Adult chooses to protect against taking responsibility for our own pain and joy is that all the things our Inner Child does to protect against being so powerless and feeling so alone create most of the pain, fear, and discomfort in our lives. Our attempts to control others and avoid being controlled, and our attempts to fill ourselves through addictions create low self-esteem, anxiety, and stress. These lead in turn to illness and magnify our feelings of aloneness, isolation, and emptiness. We generally feel internal conflict, since the Adult and Child are not working together to create harmony. We go through life feeling guilt and shame—guilt because we believe that we are *doing* something wrong and shame because we believe that there is something wrong with us as human beings.

Codependence

One of the primary negative consequences of living from the ego is a state of being that has been labeled "codependence." Codependence is a term that was coined by people working in Alcoholics Anonymous. It originally referred to the relationship between an alcoholic and the people closely involved with him or her. The term is now used to describe involvement with any addict.

A codependent is a person who is defined and controlled by other people, situations, and by the ego's "shoulds" and rules.

Codependents are defined by anything but their Higher Self. They experience their sense of self and worth *through* others. They allow others to define them, and make others responsible for their feelings. Once the internal Adult abdicates responsibility for defining and giving worth to the Inner Child, the Child is stuck looking elsewhere—being dependent on others—for definition and worth. Whenever we choose to operate from our ego, we have chosen to give away the power to define ourselves, and to give that power to others. This is the definition of a codependent—a person who gives power to others to define himself or herself.

Once we allow others to define our worth, then we must attempt to control what they think of us. All of our controlling behavior—our anger, blame, pouting, teaching, explaining, caretaking, compliance, and denial—comes from believing that we can control what others think of us and how they treat us, and that how they think of us and treat us defines us. The truth of the Higher Self is that *our sense of worth and self-esteem come from the Inner Adult loving the Inner Child.* The lie of the ego is that our worth and self-esteem come from other people.

We are systematically taught as children to believe we are responsible for the feelings of others and therefore that other people are responsible for our feelings. How often did your parents say things like "You'd better stop it or you're going to make me angry," "You're driving me crazy," "You make me so miserable," "You make me so happy"—as if we were puppeteers pulling their strings and *making* them feel and behave in a certain way? As a result of these messages we adopted the erroneous belief that other people make us happy or unhappy and that we, in turn, are responsible for others' feelings.

The abandoned Inner Child is powerless to change this belief and powerless to define itself. Only the Inner Adult has the power to change the belief and to choose to define the self. The abandoned Child is left victimized and powerless and projects this onto others, believing that if only others would change and treat him or her differently, the pain would go away. But the pain will never go away until the Inner Adult takes back the power and makes a new decision to learn with and from the Inner Child.

There are many people who connect to themselves when they are alone yet give up this connection as soon as they are around another person. People with this pattern tend to fall into two different categories: takers and caretakers. Takers are willing to take care of themselves only when another person isn't around to do it, but their primary intent is to get love, approval, and caretaking from others, believing that this is what will really make them feel good. Caretakers let go of connecting to and loving themselves around others because they believe they are responsible for giving to the other what the other wants even if it's not what they themselves want. Caretakers disconnect from themselves around others not only because they want approval from others, but because they believe they are responsible for others' feelings. They may fear that if they didn't give themselves up no one would love them and they would be alone.

Codependent Relationships

When two unrecovering codependents get together—and this is inevitable since most people are disconnected and therefore codependent—they create a codependent relationship. Both people in a codependent relationship are addicted to approval and some may be addicted to other processes (sex, work, money, and so forth) or to a substance. They are each dependent on the other's love and approval for their own good feelings and they each blame the other for their own bad feelings. They each try to control the other in overt and covert ways to get the love and approval they want. Each may want it in a different form. One may want it through sex. The other may want it through time spent together. One may want it through being taken care of financially. The other may want to be taken care of emotionally. They each try to control the other with anger, niceness, and other overt and covert strategies to get what they want. The relationship may be filled with power struggles if both resist being controlled. Power struggles are avoided only through compliance, a covert form of control.

Joel and Gretchen are a typical codependent couple. Joel is a successful businessman and Gretchen works part time as a landscape designer. Joel has an incredible knack for making money—everything he touches turns to gold, and his self-esteem is very tied to money. At home, however, Joel is a needy and demanding little boy. He has no idea how to make himself happy by himself and so expects Gretchen to be available whenever he is home. He doesn't have any friends and relies on Gretchen for all his emotional needs. In addition, he is very sexually demanding, believing that he deserves to have sex whenever he wants it because he supports the family. After all, marriage is a "give and take" proposition—he gives money, so he is entitled to take sex, and it's Gretchen's job to give it, since she takes the money. When Gretchen does not give him the time, approval, or sex he wants, Joel often gets enraged and occasionally gets physically violent. Sometimes he shows his rage by yelling and threatening Gretchen, and other times he withdraws emotionally for days at a time.

While Joel is the caretaker financially, Gretchen is the caretaker emotionally and sexually. Gretchen believes she is unimportant and undeserving, and that her worth lies in pleasing others. She has learned to use sex as a way to manipulate Joel's approval, upon which she is dependent. She hates and fears his anger and withdrawal and will do anything to avoid it, including giving herself up by spending time with him even when she would rather do something else. While Joel tries to control in overt ways, Gretchen attempts to control in covert ways, through sex, flattery, gifts, and by spending all spare time with Joel, as well as by giving up her other interests and friends. Gretchen is a reactor, believing that if only Joel were different, she wouldn't have to be so manipulative and wouldn't have to give up so much of herself.

But this is not the case, since people are always matched perfectly at the level of their common woundedness. Joel and Gretchen both operate as abandoned children in the relationship. They have each given up responsibility for their own happiness and handed it over to the other, and they each blame the other for their own unhappiness.

Most of us enter our relationships with low self-esteem, hoping our partner will make us feel whole and good about ourselves. This is one of the major difficulties in relationships, expecting our partner to be responsible for our good feelings. But it is only when we already love ourselves through loving connection with our Inner Child that we can truly love another by wanting to know that person and by supporting his or her growth and happiness. When we do not love ourselves, we are threatened by the other's growth. So instead of supporting them, we attempt to diminish and control them. When we do not know and love ourselves, we fear rejection/abandonment and domination/engulfment by our partner and find many ways to protect ourselves from our fears. A withdrawn or resistant person may touch off our fears of abandonment, so we protect ourselves by becoming controlling. A demanding or controlling person may activate our fear of being engulfed, so we protect ourselves by becoming withdrawn or resistant. We cannot give love when we are protecting ourselves from these fears. In order to have loving relationships we must first explore our Inner Child and challenge our erroneous, self-limiting beliefs about ourselves. Until we know that we are lovable, we will be dependent on others to make us feel good about ourselves, and will continue to fear being abandoned or engulfed.

The ego is always addicted to approval, which is what creates codependence, because it firmly believes that self-esteem and happiness come from others' approval. As long as we operate from this false belief, then we will continue to behave in ways that diminish our self-esteem: trying to mold ourselves into the "right" way to be, rather than being who we are; violating our own preferences to avoid disapproval (having sex when we don't want to, caretaking when we don't want to, spending money when we don't want to, entertaining guests when we don't want to); getting angry or pouting and explaining in the hopes of getting our partner to see that he or she is wrong so we can get the approval or attention we believe will make us feel good; trying to get whatever we believe we need to feel lovable (sex, connection, time with our mate or lover). Every time we behave in any of these ways that are so unloving to ourselves, we unwittingly undermine our own self-esteem. Yet at the same time our ego tells us that we must behave in these ways to get approval or be successful and avoid disapproval, rejection, and failure. Our ego constantly tells us that once we find the way to get approval or have success, then we will be happy and feel good about ourselves.

Both partners suffer greatly in codependent relationships, yet this is how most relationships function in our society. If the couple tries to get help through therapy, there is a good possibility that the therapist is an unrecovering codependent and therefore not helpful. A codependent therapist who is not in recovery cannot help others face their codependence. We cannot see in others what we have not dealt with in ourselves. Codependent therapists may even do more harm than good, since they may actually foster codependence in their clients.

Dysfunctional Families

Out of codependent relationships come dysfunctional families, that is, families where one or both parents are alcoholics, drug addicts, overeaters, workaholics, sex addicts, rage-aholics, child abusers, TV addicts, gamblers, spendthrifts, control-aholics, or caretakers. Since both parents are approval-seekers and have no clear sense of what it means to love themselves or to choose to learn, this is what they model to their children. Since they cannot love their children any more than they love themselves, the children's needs for love are not met, the child feels defective, alone, and lonely, and the ego is born within the child, starting the cycle of internal disconnection, dysfunction, and codependence all over again.

Children from alcoholic, incestuous, abusive, and other dysfunctional codependent families are hard put to know they are okay. Because they do not know that their parents' inability to love them has nothing to do with them, they naturally conclude that they are not being loved because they are somehow defective. Very early they absorb the core, shame-based ego belief that they are bad, wrong, unworthy, unlovable, unimportant, and inadequate, which sets the stage for their own internal disconnection.

Our dysfunctional society, filled with war, crime, violence, hunger, and the violation of the planet, evolves from our dysfunctional families. The cycle will not end until each of us individually decides to learn with our own Inner Child what it means to love ourselves.

CHAPTER 5

Connection

The first prerequisite of intimacy is to be intimate with oneself. As long as we are looking outside ourselves for intimacy, we will never have it and we will never be able to give it. In order to be intimate with another person, we have to know who we are, what we feel, what we think, what our values are, what is important to us, and what we want. If we do not know these things about ourselves, we can never share them with another person.

Escape From Intimacy
ANNE WILSON SCHAEF

It is easier to understand the concept of inner connection when you can experience where in your body your Child and Adult reside. The Child, the instinctual aspect, lives in the center of the body, in the solar plexus, the gut, or what is often referred to as the third *chakra* (the chakras are energy centers within the body according to Hindu tradition). When someone says, "This is my gut reaction," they are referring to the experience of the Child. When we grow up learning to trust our gut reactions, then we are very much aware of what we feel in this area of our bodies. But if we grew up denying our feelings, either because the pain of our childhood was too great and we shut down to survive, or because experiencing our truth brought too much rejection, then this area of the body may feel empty, dead, or numb. In other cases, people may continue to feel many different feelings in this area but never really pay attention to what these feelings are saying, because they have been taught to mistrust their feelings or gut reactions.

The thought processes of the Adult reside in the head. The loving Adult, the Adult who has chosen to learn, is an energy circle that moves between the head and the heart, the fourth chakra. This means that the thoughts of the loving Adult are filled with love and compassion flowing from the heart. Because this heart channel is open, the Adult can easily move its attention into the third chakra, the feelings of the Child, in order to know about and learn from those feelings. When this occurs, a continuous circle of energy is created between the head, heart, and gut. This is the inner connection. The Adult is experiencing the feelings of the Child and is open to knowing, understanding, and acting on them, while the Child feels the love, support, and knowledge of the Adult. The heart is open to giving and receiving with others because it is open to the Self.

The unloving Adult, the Adult who has chosen to protect itself from pain, fear, discomfort, and responsibility for the Child, disconnects from the heart. When the intent is to protect, the heart may constrict and feel tight, or it may just feel empty. With the heart closed down, there is no access to the Child, and the Child is abandoned.

Defining *Connection*

We all yearn for deep emotional and spiritual connection to another person. Connection is the feeling of wholeness and unity that we have within ourselves when we are in harmony with the Inner Child, and the feeling of oneness we have with others when each person is open to his or her own Child and therefore open to others. Connection is an unbroken circle of love energy that occurs between the Adult and the Child, between the Higher Selves of two or more people, and between an individual's Higher Self and the universal God/Goddess energy. Connection with oneself brings a sense of peace and joy. Connection with others and the universe is a feeling of intense peace and joy. In fact, it is the most wonderful feeling we can ever experience. It is what love is all about.

Many people attempt to attain a sense of connection with God or the universe through meditation. Whether or not they attain this depends upon the *intent* of the meditation. When the intent is to learn, then meditation, especially when involving concentration on the breath, can open you to experiencing your Inner Child. One way people cut off the feelings of the Child is through shallow breathing or by holding the breath. When the intent is to know yourself, the breath can help you. As you connect more and more with your Inner Child and your heart opens, you feel the universal God/Goddess connection. But if your intent is to bypass your inner work and go directly to connection with God, not only will you never get there, but the meditation itself is then being used as a form of addiction—attempting to get your good feelings from outside of yourself. We have worked with people who have meditated for years and are no closer to connection than they were the day they started, because their intent is to avoid responsibility for themselves. They use meditation as a way to remain separate from their Inner Child. Universal connection is attained only through the Higher Self, the inner connection between the Adult and the Child.

The more you connect with your Inner Child, the more you will naturally experience universal connection, a profound state where you feel love and universal wisdom flowing into you. This transcendent experience is available to anyone willing to do the necessary recovery work.

Connection with Others

Women often have a sense of connection in their friendships with each other, yet feel frustrated in their attempts to connect with the men in their lives. This is because our culture has discouraged men from owning their feminine aspect, their Inner Child, just as it has discouraged women from owning their masculine aspect, their Adult.

If we examine the friendships of men and women, we find that men often share dialogue involving intellectual discussions about work, politics, or sports, dialogue that comes from the Adult. Close women friends, however, often delve into deep discussions involving feelings and beliefs, sharing themselves and learning through the curiosity of the Child. Their relationships are generally on a much deeper level. Often men find this sense of connection only with women. Women, however, sometimes find this connection difficult with men, because men may lack awareness of the feelings that come from the Child. We frequently hear our women clients say, "I wish I could talk to my husband the way I talk to my women friends. It seems so easy to connect with my friends and so hard to connect with my husband. It seems strange to say it, but I feel more intimate with my women friends than with my husband! He seems to have such a hard time sharing his feelings with me or really understanding what I feel." In our experience, however, this is changing as more and more men are opening to their feelings.

All of us want connection with others probably more than we want anything else. But many people believe that such connection must be given to them by another person, and therefore connection eludes them. It is only when we are open to our own Child that we are open to connection with others. When we are in our egos, it is as if we close the door to that circle of love energy. Then, because we feel so separate and empty, we try to manipulate a connection with others through control or compliance. We might "act" nice or loving as a way to get connection, never realizing that we first have to connect to our own

Child before the door will open. Once the door opens, then we feel loving, and our behavior is an honest reflection of our feelings, rather than just an act.

Connection Happens in the Moment

Inner connection, the experience of wholeness and oneness of the Higher Self, occurs whenever our Adult is in loving dialogue with our Child. The ego, with its sense of separation within, takes over whenever our Adult chooses unloving inner dialogue, or when our Adult leaves the Child to deal with things by itself.

The ego exists in the past and the future. When we are in our ego, we are projecting our beliefs from the past into the future. That is what causes fear and anxiety. We become frightened and anxious when we think something bad is going to happen—we are going to fail, be rejected, be wrong, be laughed at, or lose someone we love, and we believe we can't handle such painful feelings. We cannot connect with others from our egos because when we are in our egos we are disconnected from ourselves. We cannot connect when we are frightened or anxious, because we cannot connect unless we are completely in the moment. When we are in the moment we are in our Higher Self.

When we are attached to the outcome of an interaction, we are not in the moment. When our goal is to *make* a connection happen, or our expectation is to have fun or have sex, or to be loved, or get approval, or avoid disapproval, then we are not in the moment, we are in the future. Anytime we try to get something or make something happen we are in the future, in our egos. Therefore, if a goal or an expectation exists between two people, there can be no true connection, just manipulations. True connection with another occurs only when both people are completely in the moment with their feelings and with each other. If one or the other of them is attached to the outcome, then their thoughts are future-oriented, as they try to achieve that goal, and they lose touch with themselves and the other person in that moment. You can't be aware of what you're feeling or what the other person is feeling if you are worried about whether or not your desired outcome will happen. And if you have an expectation of sex, approval, or connection, then all of your behavior is an attempt to get what you want and is therefore a manipulation.

It's always easier to be open to the moment and to connect in a love affair than it is to connect in a committed relationship. Once people move into a committed relationship or get married their fears of disapproval, rejection, and domination become activated. In our first primary relationships, those with our parents, we all developed fears of disapproval, rejection, and domination, and we bring these fears with us into all subsequent primary relationships, until we confront them and work through them. For many people, these fears do not get touched off in an affair because the fear of loss is not as great. Therefore, people often connect more deeply in affairs than in their primary relationship.

Sex and Connection

One of the main misunderstandings between men and women occurs around the area of sexuality. Many of the couples we work with come into our offices with the same complaint: he wants more sex and she does not. The issue is generally the same—a lack of emotional and spiritual connection.

Many men, though certainly not all, use sex as a way to connect, yet most women do not feel sexual until there is a connection. This presents a dilemma for many couples because the man is saying, "If we make love, then I'll feel open and connected to you," and the woman is saying "But I don't feel like having sex until you are open and we connect." In addition, many people use sex as a way to be affirmed, as a way to feel good about themselves. This constitutes a sexual addiction, since they believe that their good feelings come from being attractive to the other person and having sex with them. The person at the other end of this addiction often feels pressured to *make* his or her partner happy. There is no possibility of connection with this type of interaction. Both people end up feeling bad, not understanding why connection cannot occur.

Sexuality can come from either the ego or the Higher Self. Sex from the ego always takes place with the intent to *get* something—to get love, connection, affirmation, release from tension, orgasm. Sex from the Higher Self is always an expression of love and is therefore a *giving* response. Sometimes this is confusing, as when a man who wants to make love says to a woman who doesn't, "But I just want to love you. You are not letting me love you." This is the kind of confusing statement that can lead a woman to feel crazy. He says he wants to love her, yet it doesn't *feel* that way to her. Clearly, if he really wanted to love her, he would not want her to make love, or do anything else, if she didn't want to. Instead, he would want to know what she did want, and would truly feel good giving her what she wanted. Whenever a man tries to talk a woman into making love, he is in his ego and is trying to get something, even if he says it's because he loves her. This is equally true if the roles are reversed and a woman is doing the talking.

Sex from the Higher Self is always a very sensual experience. When couples make love from the Higher Self, they do not have to be taught. When they naturally express their loving feelings for each other, everything between them flows. People have sexual problems when the fears and beliefs of the ego enter the relationship and they make love from their abandoned Child. The moment the sexual energy changes from giving to getting, there are problems. Even if a person is in a giving mode while making love, but in a taking mode in the rest of the relationship, this will be reflected in the sexual relationship. But when both people are open to each other from their Higher Self, and when they have established the love/energy connection, then their sexuality will flow naturally and freely. That is why trying to solve sexual problems by changing behavior rarely works. It is only when the intent changes from getting to giving and a true connection occurs that sexual problems are truly resolved. The following example of this was written by Sheila, one of our clients.

Sex had always been a problem for me. For years I believed there was something wrong with me. My first marriage ended because I never felt like having sex, and I was sure it was all my fault. My second marriage, a long one, was the same way, but I stuck it out because I figured that this was the most I could hope for. Then I met Wayne. We met casually at work, and slowly became friends. We started spending more time together, each of us sharing the most intimate of details about ourselves. It wasn't just the talking—my husband and I have always talked a lot and shared intimate conversation. It's hard to explain, but it's as if he opened a door inside of him and let me into himself in a deep, feeling way, and he also stepped through the door I opened for him. His energy was open to me in the moment in a way I had never experienced. We knew each other a couple of years before we finally made love, but when we did it was like nothing I'd ever experienced. Both of us found ourselves loving to do things that we never liked to do before, like kiss a lot. We could spend hours just kissing! And our bodies seemed to fit together so well. Now we find that little defects that in another person would have bothered us don't bother us at all. He even does some of the things that drove me crazy with my husband—like forgetting things—but with him they don't bother me at all. And everything we do together is fun, even things like shopping for furniture, which I always hated doing in the past. I've realized that it's not what we do that makes the difference, but the energy with which we do it. When the energy between us is open and flowing with love, then everything works. I now realize that with both of my husbands I didn't feel turned on because there was no real connection. They never really opened themselves to me, so I couldn't really feel them, and they never extended their energy into me. Even their giving felt like taking because there were always strings attached. Wayne never gets mad if I don't want to do something, even if I don't want to make love. He just stays open to knowing me. It feels so wonderful!

All problems in marriages and families stem from the internal disconnection. Since we cannot love and connect to others until we love and connect to ourselves, learning to love the Inner Child is the key to resolving relationship problems.

CHAPTER 6

The Results of Connection

The combination of these two powers, the reasoning one, dependent on learning, and the instinctive one, finely versed in the same
sort of innate knowledge that guides other animals through their
entire lives—the results of their interplay—is the human character
and the uniquely human potential for intellectually refined,
instinctual efficiency.

The Continuum Concept
JEAN LIEDLOFF

When we choose to live in a connected way with our Inner Child,
transforming the ego into the Higher Self, life becomes a wonderful
experience. We feel peaceful, centered, and physically healthy, with a
sense of wholeness within and a sense of compassion and oneness with
all living beings. We feel joyful, even when we are sad. As Richard, one
of our clients said, "The pain I feel when I'm disconnected is awful. But
when I connect with my Inner Child, even feeling his pain feels good."

Self-Esteem

The more deeply we learn to love our Inner Child, the more we
experience high self-esteem. Self-esteem simply means feeling lovable,
adequate, and worthwhile. While our ego tells us that self-esteem
comes from others' approval, the truth is that self-esteem comes from
inner approval, *from what the Inner Adult thinks about the Inner Child, and
how the Adult treats the Child.* When others give us approval, we may
feel good for the moment, but the good feeling soon goes away, and we
need more approval to feel good again (which is what makes it an
addiction—we need more and more of it to feel good). Good feelings
from the ego are always short-lived. But when the Inner Adult loves
the Inner Child over a period of time, the Child comes to know that it
is lovable and worthwhile. This knowledge is not momentary, but deep
and permanent.

The more time you spend being a loving Adult and learning about your Inner Child, the more you will like and value being with yourself. When you find that you like being with yourself more than with anyone else, then you are no longer addicted to anyone. That is not to say that you always want to be alone—far from it. When you fill yourself up by being in touch with and loving yourself, then you feel so full of love that you naturally want to offer it to others. A connected person does not seek a relationship in order to get something, but rather to give love to others as they've given love to themselves. "Love thy neighbor as thyself," means that first you must love yourself and then you can love others as you love yourself. If you love being with others but you don't love being with yourself, it means that you value others more than you value yourself, and that you want to be with them to get something from them, rather than to give something to them. You are being needy and addicted when this is the case. When you spend enough time learning with your Inner Child, you will eventually see and know who you are to such an extent that you love being with yourself. This is high self-esteem.

High self-esteem is a choice. It is the consequence of how we feel about ourselves, what we choose to believe about ourselves, whether we choose to believe we are lovable or unlovable. When we realize that high self-esteem comes from loving our own Inner Child rather than through others' approval, then we can see that we do indeed have choice about how we feel about ourselves. As we become nonshaming and nonviolating toward ourselves and others, loving our Inner Child and others unconditionally, the hardness that we used to believe we needed to protect ourselves from hurt melts into a sense of softness and inner power.

Personal Power and Softness

Softness is the energy of warmth, tenderness, love, and power that emanates from people when they are in their Higher Selves. At this moment they know and love themselves, do not shame or violate themselves and others, do not seek approval nor fear disapproval, are not self-conscious, and do not take personally others' criticism, anger, or rejection. Soft energy radiates from personal power, for when people know who they are, what they want, and how they feel, and they know they have the right to want what they want and feel what they feel, then they cannot be dominated, controlled, or emotionally hurt by others. When we are in this state of owning our personal power we are beyond weakness, and beyond violence of any kind. We can afford to be soft because we know we are not weak. Being in this state is an ideal, something we can all strive to be in more of the time. Unfortunately, many people, when reading the word *soft* or hearing someone refer to softness, think of a marshmallow, a wimp, a jerk, a nerd, or a nebbish. Obviously, there is much confusion between softness and weakness.

Softness versus Weakness

Our ego has taught us to believe that softness and power are mutually exclusive, that softness is weakness and hardness is powerful. The ego tells us, therefore, that we cannot be soft and powerful at the same time. But to give and receive love we must be soft. Love never comes from the hardness of the ego.

It's very important to understand the difference between softness and weakness. We are weak when we are passive, giving ourselves up to others and allowing them to take advantage of us. We are also inwardly weak when we fear being controlled by others and cover this fear over by attempting to control others. We are weak when we give power to others' approval and disapproval. We are weak anytime we are afraid and allow that fear to control us in any way, whether by getting angry, critical, blaming, or passive, compliant, or resistant. In other words, we are weak whenever we are disconnected from our Inner Child, abdicating responsibility for ourselves and acting from the fears and beliefs of the ego.

Soft, then, does not mean weak, and it does not mean compliance. Take Joe, for example. He is a typical union contract negotiator. He comes to the bargaining table armed with demands and causes and threats. He attempts to overpower his opposition with hardness and unavailability. He must say "no" with all the thunder he can muster. What if, however, he simply and softly said, from an inwardly connected place, "These are my terms." He could then sit back and stay centered within himself and not have to put his spirit and body through the tortures of tension and hardness. He can leave that to his opposition, who will eventually wear themselves down. From his inner connection he can see the misery of his opponent and still love him for his struggle. This is power *and* is softness—the power of softness.

One day Erika observed the following interaction between a friend of hers and an acquaintance of his. They were sitting around talking at a picnic when her friend lit a cigarette. She knew that he wanted to quit smoking but was having difficulty doing so. His acquaintance started to lecture him about smoking and asked how he could continue to do such a thing. Her friend, a soft and sensitive man, smiled and said simply, "We all have our bad habits, don't we?" He didn't get angry or defensive or try to explain anything. He stayed soft and centered, yet did not get overrun by the other man. Had this man felt wrong for smoking, had he been judgmental towards himself or fearful of others' disapproval, then he probably would have felt hurt by the criticism and been defensive, or he would have said nothing but been inwardly upset or angry. His self-judgments would have made him weak. Instead, his acceptance of himself, and therefore of the other person, made him soft and powerful.

Softness and Power

Softness is the way we are when we are connected and unafraid, which is the most powerful way to be. Pseudo power, the power to dominate and control others, is based on fear, and is often how the abandoned Child attempts to control others and avoid being controlled. It is manipulative and never creates joy or self-esteem. True power, which is the power to nurture and give, rather than dominate and take, is soft.

Marcia, a client of ours who is in her early fifties and in a second marriage, wrote the following about the power of softness.

In my psychology class this week we were asked to pair off into couples and do an exercise. The men were asked to make a fist and resist opening it. The women were instructed to get the fist open in whatever way they could.

As I turned and faced the young man next to me whom I had known only through casual interaction in class, I knew intuitively what I needed to do. I looked deeply but softly into his eyes and then rolled up his shirt sleeve. I then gently stroked his arm up and down, as I often did with my children when they were tense. Then I proceeded to stroke his fingers and open one finger at a time, all the while looking softly into his eyes. His fist opened without any resistance. The young man smiled and seemed momentarily transformed. He didn't know exactly what had happened, but said that he felt great. I too felt great, not like I had won because I had succeeded in opening his fist, but because I felt warm and closer to him. His fist had been opened through the power of softness.

The teacher was very surprised to hear our experience because, as he expected, most of the women had attempted with clenched teeth to pry their partner's fist open, meeting with great resistance and occasional failure.

I have spent nearly ten years in my marriage trying to pry my husband open with force. It has never worked. Hardness and force have been met only with resistance, anger, and alienation. Just as anger was about to shut us down forever, I was able with the help of therapy to get in touch with that soft place inside that wants to love.

I have had to pay attention and stay conscious all the time of when I'm connected and giving and when I'm disconnected and forcing. I find it all too easy to shift from giving to being judgmental and demanding, from being soft and open to being hard and closed.

In the past I have been very judgmental about my husband, especially about his missing work. I was suspicious when he said he was sick, and I was angry when he was depressed. This week he had minor surgery and missed some work. Staying in touch with my softness, I was able to accept his absence from work without making judgments and without worrying about money, his reputation at work, or about his reasons for staying home. He didn't seem concerned, so I chose not to be, and the tension this situation has always caused did not arise. I was free to remain in touch with my positive feelings and to feel loving towards him.

Genuine softness is powerful because it expects nothing in return. It is self-empowering, so I am not at those moments tied to the concern about what I'm going to get in return, which limits giving and makes it conditional. And, amazingly enough, this kind of giving usually has a very positive impact. Because it is so free, it creates a loving circle, a flow of loving feelings between us.

On a number of occasions this week I said or did small things, like noticing the way he looked, touching him more, asking about his health, and generally expressing myself in a more loving way. He also seemed to be softer and more open.

On other occasions he responded with a touch of his old anger, apprehension, or suspicion. Knowing that I had intended to be soft and unjudgmental, knowing that he was reacting defensively because of the history between us, I was able to remain soft, and I felt great. Within a few moments he had apologized and acknowledged that his reactions had been protective. Of course, I too have become very conscious of my reactions and am able to quickly explore them with him.

This is a breakthrough for us, although there is much more work and healing to be done. But once you discover how it feels to be soft, once you see the powerful effect it can have on your relationship with yourself and others, you don't mind doing whatever it takes to be that way all the time.

Historically, we have loved truly soft and powerful people, but they have generally met with disaster—people like Gandhi, or Martin Luther King, or Jesus Christ. These people met hardness in response to their softness and innocence. The human ego is determined to destroy softness, secretly fearing its power; the ego is afraid of anything that threatens its control over us. Why then would anyone be motivated to be soft? The answer is because hardness does not bring anyone joy. You can be hard and unloving, or you can be joyous.

What about the risk of being annihilated by those who are hard and acting from their egos? Until now, most of us have believed that the only way we can safely respond to hardness is by protecting ourselves with our own hardness. *That is the belief of the ego.* If it is true that there is no power greater than love, then the most powerful way we can respond is with softness. It is also the only response that will enhance our self-esteem and bring us joy. If at this point you are shaking your head and saying, "Not me, I don't want to get obliterated by people," then your ego is seducing you into believing that your hardness is effective in protecting you against the hardness of others.

The ego wants us to believe that when attacked, we must counterattack. Yet all we accomplish when we do this is create war—in families, in our society, and in the world. It is true that in the past, when one nation or society was attacked by another, those who did not fight back or who did not have adequate weapons were overrun by those with more "powerful" weapons (powerful in the sense of power over others). But if we continue to operate on that basis today we will wipe ourselves out. So it is time to move from the hard power of the ego into the soft power of the Higher Self. We know, however, that the ego will not give up its dominance easily.

A Course in Miracles states that "The ego is . . . particularly likely to attack you when you react lovingly, because it has evaluated you as unloving, and you are going against its judgment." This means that your ego believes that you are an unloving person and as long as you believe that, your ego has control over you. If, however, you awaken to the fact that you are loving and lovable, the ego will attack you because it fears the loss of power over you. Your ego has spent your life convincing you that you must be hard to be powerful. We've yet to learn that the most powerful defense is the defenselessness of softness and love.

Ted told Margie the following story in one of his therapy sessions.

I've got this boss who has been on my back for a long time. Whenever he doesn't understand something or something goes wrong, he comes yelling at me. I've always hated this, and I've always reacted by yelling back at him. Fortunately, he doesn't have the authority to fire me, but what has always happened is that we have a sort of cold war that often goes on for weeks after one of these blow-ups. It's very uncomfortable for both of us, and the problems never get resolved. Last week, after you and I talked about my Adult showing up for my Child, he again came yelling at me, and then went stomping off to his office. But this time, instead of following him into his office, yelling at him, and telling him off, I went in and sat down quietly, inwardly telling my Child that I would handle this for him. I decided to be curious and to learn more about the situation, instead of being angry. So I asked him gently what was upsetting him so much. He calmed down immediately, and we had the first good talk we've ever had. We even began to resolve some of the things that had been upsetting him! It was great! Instead of ending up feeling angry and frustrated and helpless, I ended up feeling calm and powerful. I always thought I had to be tough to get what I wanted and not be pushed around, but I can begin to see that all that's gotten me is upset and frustrated. Now that the door is open to talk, I have the feeling that we can resolve whatever other problems come up. I had been feeling so upset at work that I was thinking of transferring, but now I'm liking my job a whole lot better! It's hard to believe that something as simple as responding calmly and curiously from my Adult instead of angrily from my abandoned Child can be so powerful!

Eve, in one of her sessions with Erika, reported the following experience with her husband, Jack, and their nineteen-year-old son, Bret, who was home on vacation from college.

When Bret first came home, Jack had given him a list of things that he wanted Bret to get done while he was home. Two nights before Bret was leaving for school, it became apparent that the chores weren't going to get done. We were sitting around the dinner table talking and Jack brought it up. Bret got a little defensive, and suddenly Jack was yelling at him, telling him he was selfish and ungrateful and that he felt taken advantage of by Bret. He told Bret that if he couldn't help around the house then he shouldn't bother coming home. Bret yelled back, saying "Fine with me. I don't like being here anyway." At this point I brought my Adult in and decided to try to understand what was going on, so I said quietly to Bret, "Honey, there must be a good reason that you don't want to help around here. I think of you as a giving person, yet you don't seem to want to give here. Do you have any idea why?" "Actually, I've been thinking about that a lot," he said. "I'm not totally sure of all the reasons, but I think it has something to do with feeling controlled. When other people ask me to do things, it makes me feel good to help them, but I also know that I can say no and they won't be mad at me. But when you guys ask me to do things, you're not really asking, you're demanding, and I don't like that."

After that the three of us spent the next hour talking. It was one of the best talks we've ever had! Bret has always been such an inward kid. It's always been so hard to get him to talk. Yet when I asked him what was going on in a soft and loving way, he opened up so easily. I really loved talking to him like that! And since he's been back at school, we've continued to have good conversations.

Eve is discovering how very powerful softness is and how gratifying her interactions can be when the intent is to love and learn rather than to protect herself with her anger or criticism or threats.

Terry Dobson, author of *Giving in to Get Your Way*, tells the following moving story about himself.

The train clanked and rattled through the suburbs of Tokyo on a drowsy spring afternoon. Our car was comparatively empty—a few housewives with their kids in tow, some old folks going shopping. I gazed absently at the drab houses and dusty hedgerows.

At one station the doors opened and suddenly the afternoon quiet was shattered by a man bellowing violent incomprehensible curses. The man staggered into our car. He wore laborer's clothing, and he was big, drunk, and dirty. Screaming, he swung at a woman holding a baby. The blow sent her spinning into the laps of an elderly couple. It was a miracle that the baby was unharmed.

Terrified, the couple jumped up and scrambled towards the other end of the car. The laborer aimed a kick at the retreating back of the old woman but missed as she scuttled to safety. This so enraged the drunk that he grabbed the metal pole in the center of the car and tried to wrench it out of its stanchion. I could see that one of his hands was cut and bleeding. The train lurched ahead, the passengers frozen with fear. I stood up.

I was young then, some twenty years ago, and in pretty good shape. I had been putting in a solid eight hours of aikido training nearly every day for the past three years. I liked to throw and grapple. The trouble was my martial skill was untested in actual combat. As students of aikido we were not allowed to fight.

"Aikido," my teacher had said again and again, "is the art of reconciliation. Whoever has the mind to fight has broken his connection with the universe. If you try to dominate people, you're already defeated. We study how to resolve conflict, not how to start it."

I listened to his words. I tried very hard. I even went so far as to cross the street to avoid the *chimpera*, the pinball punks who lounged around the train stations. My forbearance exalted me. I felt both tough and holy. In my heart, however, I wanted an absolutely legitimate opportunity whereby I might save the innocent by destroying the guilty.

"This is it!" I said to myself as I got to my feet. "People are in danger. If I don't do something fast, somebody probably will get hurt."

Seeing me stand up, the drunk recognized the chance to focus his rage. "Aha!" he roared. "A foreigner! You need a lesson in Japanese manners!"

I held on lightly to the commuter strap overhead and gave him a slow look of disgust and dismissal. I planned to take this turkey apart, but he had to make the first move. I wanted him mad, so I pursed my lips and blew him an insolent kiss.

"All right!" he hollered, "You're going to get a lesson." He gathered himself for a rush at me.

A fraction of a second before he could move, someone shouted "Hey!" It was earsplitting. I remember the strangely joyous lilting quality of it—as though you and a friend had been searching diligently for something and he had suddenly stumbled upon it. "Hey!"

I wheeled to my left; the drunk spun to his right. We both stared down at a little old Japanese man. He must have been well into his seventies, this tiny gentleman sitting there immaculate in his kimono. He took no notice of me but beamed delightedly at the laborer, as though he had a most important, most welcome secret to share.

"C'mere," the old man said in easy vernacular, beckoning to the drunk. "C'mere and talk with me!" He waved his hand lightly.

The big man followed as if on a string. He planted his feet belligerently in front of the old gentleman and roared above the clacking wheels, "Why the hell should I talk to you?" The drunk now had his back to me. If his elbow moved so much as a millimeter, I'd drop him in his socks.

The old man continued to beam at the laborer. "What'cha been drinkin'?" he asked, his eyes sparkling with interest. "I been drinkin' sake" the laborer bellowed, "and it's none of your business." Flecks of spittle spattered the old man.

"Oh, that's wonderful!" the old man said, "absolutely wonderful! You see, I love sake too. Every night, me and my wife (she's seventy-six, you know), we warm up a little bottle of sake and we take it into the garden and we sit on our old wooden bench. We watch the sun go down and we look to see how our persimmon tree is doing. My great-grandfather planted that tree, and we worry about whether it will recover from those ice storms we had last winter. Our tree has done better than I expected, though, especially when you consider the poor quality of the soil. It's gratifying to watch, when we take our sake and go out to enjoy the evening—even when it rains!" He looked up at the laborer, his eyes twinkling.

As he struggled to follow the old man's conversation, the drunk's face began to soften. His fists slowly unclenched. "Yeah," he said. "I love persimmons too . . ." His voice trailed off.

"Yes," said the old man smiling, "and I'm sure you have a wonderful wife."

"No," replied the laborer, "my wife died." Very gently, swaying with the motion of the train, the big man began to sob. "I don't got no *wife*. I don't got no *home*. I don't got no *job*. I'm so *ashamed* of myself." Tears rolled down his cheeks; a spasm of despair rippled through his body.

Now it was my turn. Standing in my well-scrubbed youthful innocence, my make-this-world-safe-for-democracy righteousness, I suddenly felt dirtier than he was.

The train arrived at my stop. As the doors opened I heard the old man cluck sympathetically. "My, my," he said, "that is a difficult predicament indeed. Sit down here, and tell me about it."

I turned my head for one last look. The laborer was sprawled on the seat, his head in the old man's lap. The old man was softly stroking the filthy matted hair.

As the train pulled away I sat down on a bench. What I had wanted to do with muscle had been accomplished with love.

Discovering the Power of Passion

One of the secrets to having a happy life is to find your passion. Passion means totally immersing yourself in an experience that you find very compelling for the purpose of expression, play, and learning. It means physically, emotionally, intellectually, and spiritually learning about something and creating with it. It is the thing you love that puts the "Wow!" into your life. Discovering your passion or passions leads you toward feelings of self-worth and away from addictions. When you have a passion in your life, nothing can take it away from you. It is not a luxury to pursue this experience, but a necessity, for without that special experience that gives meaning to our lives, we tend to wander about aimlessly looking for someone, something, or some substance to fill the void within us. Your ego will do anything to keep you from connecting to this very empowering experience. It will tell you that you have no time or money, or that you're incapable, or that there is nothing out there that will ever really interest you and so there is no point in looking for it.

Some people have found passion in physical activities or sports, and others have found their passion in the arts or other creative experiences. Some do these activities, but have found no passion, because they use them as addictions to fill their emptiness, rather than as creative expressions of their aliveness. Still others have no idea where to begin. The place to begin is with your Inner Child.

Your Inner Child is the passionate aspect of you. It is the Child within that can tell you what your true interests are. As you spend more and more time learning with and from your Inner Child, you will naturally tune into your passions. Your Child has the answer and has probably been telling you all along. How often do you hear yourself say, "I'd like to try that one day," or "Some day I'm going to . . ." The truth is, we often say these things but rarely act on them. The only way for you to discover your passion is to keep trying different paths and to be open to your Inner Child as you try them. Children are naturally passionate about many things: dance lessons, art, music, reading, building things, rock collecting, stamp collecting, acting, sports, creative play. As they grow, they are often put down for their passion and intensity, or their interests are belittled. Was there a passion in your life that you long ago gave up?

Passion may or may not be a part of your work. It is wonderful to do work we are passionate about and enjoy, and all of us can move ourselves in that direction, but until we bring that about, we can work to support our passions. This gives our work more meaning and our lives a joyous focus.

Many of the people we work with are struggling to find their passion. One woman, Beverly, shared the following experience with us.

I used to do crafts as a child, and I really loved it. I'd gotten back into doing it and it was lots of fun. But in talking with my Inner Child recently, I discovered that what she really wanted was to learn to draw. The Adult part of me had decided long ago that I couldn't draw, that I had to just stick with crafts, but I decided to try it and see what happened. I signed up for a "Drawing on the Right Side of the Brain" class, and I can't believe how much fun I'm having! It was hard at first because my ego kept telling me that everyone else would be better than me and that I would be embarrassed. But finally my loving Adult took over and told my Child that it didn't matter what others thought, that we were just here to have fun, and that I would love her no matter how she drew. Well! Imagine my surprise when I found out I could actually draw! My Child is so delighted that I took this risk and that I gave her the freedom to fail. I'm wondering how many other things I can do that I never thought were possible.

Beverly made a conscious choice to open to her Inner Child. She has tried many activities in much the same way. Each experience was filled with learning and joy, and each experience encouraged her to another. These experiences will eventually lead her to her passion.

We believe that one of the reasons so many teenagers turn to drugs is out of boredom. We've noticed that those teenagers whose lives are filled with exciting, creative, and learning activities have little time left for alcohol and drugs. In other words, those teenagers, and adults as well, who are connected with the joy and delight of their Child, who experience excitement and passion in their lives, and whose primary intent is to learn and create rather than to avoid responsibility for their boredom, pain, and joy, have no need for addictions or escapes.

Once you become aware of your Child's passions, it is up to you as a loving Adult to act on them, and not to let your fears of failure get in the way. If your Inner Child wants to paint, it is up to you to buy the paints and set up the time and place, even though you may be afraid that you can't do it. Acting in your Child's behalf in spite of your fears is essential if you are to love and support your Child. So if your Child wants to learn to play the piano, it is up to the Adult in you to buy or rent a piano and find a teacher. If your Child wants to build things out of wood, it is up to the Adult in you to set up the time and place and buy the materials. If your Child wants to learn to sail, it is up to you to make the phone call to set up the lessons. If your Child wants to collect rocks, it is up to you to take him or her rock collecting. It is also up to the Adult in you not to judge your Child's passions, but to support them in any way you can. As Joseph Campbell says, "Follow your bliss." Follow the bliss, the passion within your Inner Child, and you will discover your joy.

You have an Inner Child and will always have one. You can go through your life denying your Child and closing it in a mental closet, or you can go through life hand in hand with that part of you that is your joy and sadness, as well as your creativity, passion, and softness. The development of passion is a natural outgrowth of doing your inner healing. If you have not yet discovered your passion, have patience. As the woundedness of your unloved Child gets healed through your loving re-parenting, your passion will emerge.

Loving Relationships

We can have what we want—high self-esteem, personal power, aliveness and passion, and loving relationships—only as we move toward unconditionally loving ourselves and others. Loving our Inner Child leads to loving others, which leads to loving relationships. The following diagram illustrates this:

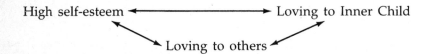

To love another, you must love yourself. It is at those moments when you do love and accept yourself that you are in your Higher Self and able to love another. Being loving to others is an act of *self* love, because it makes you happy and raises your own self-esteem.

In order to love another, you must be willing to make yourself happy by being aware of and acting in behalf of the needs of both your Adult and your Child. When you make another responsible for your happiness, you also tend to blame that person for your unhappiness. You are not being loving toward other people when you are blaming them for your own unhappiness. Once we take responsibility for our own happiness and behave in loving ways toward ourselves, then we are able to love others.

Love is purely a function of the Higher Self. The Higher Self *is* love and *wants* to love, while the ego is only concerned with getting love and avoiding pain. We can be afraid and in pain and still love, but we cannot *protect ourselves* from feeling and being responsible for our fear and pain and still love. A mother who loves her child and protects it from an intruder or rescues it from a burning building is expressing love despite her fear. Yet the same mother may respond to her child's poor grades by being afraid that she is a bad mother and may then protect herself by blaming the child or punishing it. Although she loves her child, when her fear takes charge, she disconnects from her Inner Child and is unloving toward her son or daughter. We make the choice to love or not, to be disconnected and in our ego, or to be connected and in our Higher Self, every second that we live. When we feel afraid, we may choose to protect ourselves by disconnecting, but we can just as often choose to love, even though we are afraid or hurt. This is a goal that we continually move toward when we choose to learn with our Inner Child and to explore and challenge the false beliefs of our ego. If we were able to be loving every moment, we would be truly enlightened beings. But we are not—we are just lovably human.

Life presents all of us with many situations that challenge our ability to be loving: a friend may be late, your lover may not want to make love when you do, your mate may spend money on something that you consider frivolous, he or she may have an affair, or your child may get bad grades or take drugs. When you have done your inner work and have learned to love the Child within you, you will naturally respond to others in loving ways no matter what the problem, thereby creating loving relationships in your life.

Dave, a client of ours, wrote the following, which he entitled "Self-Awareness and the Inner Child."

My self-awareness work began in August 1975 when I first took est. Since that time, until recently, I've pursued this form of growth, interrupted only by job-related activities. The joy of being briefly connected to myself led to an attachment to est, in spite of the various warnings.

Almost all of us involved in est could tell one another how to *be*—we were enlightened! Eventually, tired of spreading the word and confronting others unwilling to grow, I stopped for a hard look at my own growth. From listening to the responses of people with whom I shared my enlightened experiences, I realized I had gotten stalled. I was preoccupied with the thought that I still hadn't resolved some major personal conflicts, although outwardly I seemed to have all the right answers.

Determined to resolve these issues, I committed to a period of highly intense participation in bigger and more expensive programs. At times I felt terrific. And of course there was more and more data to consume. However, I made very little progress toward coping with major issues in my personal life. Eventually I reached a crisis.

I could remain connected and present at work, but I became disconnected when I encountered problems with my relationships. I had nothing to guide me; I simply did not know what I wanted. After many hours with Dr. Margie Paul, I can now see that there was a major conflict between my Inner Child and my Adult. I believe most self-awareness programs suffer a breakdown here.

By working with my Inner Child, listening with the intent to learn, and acting in behalf of both my Child and my Adult, I have resolved most of my deeply ingrained personal issues. This work is the missing piece that led to the dissatisfaction I had experienced earlier. It is a fundamental process that can lead to real change and altered behavior patterns. Up to now most programs have taught awareness and responsibility and the acceptance of behavior patterns that my Adult had to continue to cope with. My Inner Child had no effective means of communication, so I couldn't learn from it. Now, feeling good can last, and it's entirely up to me, no one else.

CHAPTER 7

Discovering the Loving Inner Adult

The ideal role of the Inner Parent is to love, support, and nurture
the Inner Child. It is able to accept, love, and nurture the Inner
Child while still having a sense of the Inner Child being a separate
and distinct Self. The ideal Inner Parent does not feel it "owns" the
Inner Child any more than an outer parent should feel he or she
"owns" an outer child.

Self-Parenting
DR. JOHN K. POLLARD, III

The primary failure in our culture is the lack of adequate role modeling
for a loving Inner Adult. The media have not provided it, and few of
us had parents who were connected to their Inner Child from their
loving Inner Adult, so our parents did not provide that role modeling
either. They were unloving to themselves and therefore unloving to us,
and our own Inner Adult is patterned after that unloving model.

Yet all of us have an Inner Child who knows exactly what it wants
and needs to feel loved. We are born knowing about love and about
how right and good it feels, and we know deep within us when it is not
there. We have been systematically taught to mistrust that knowledge,
so we have learned to disregard the messages from our Child. When
we choose to learn, we open the door to learning about love.

The problem is that our Inner Child may not teach us about love
right away because it may not trust us. It may feel too vulnerable to
say, "This is how I want to be loved by you," when it has rarely felt
loved by you at all. Your Inner Child might not speak to you much
until it feels loved, so it is up to the Adult part of you to discover how
to truly love your Inner Child.

Most of us have learned more about unloving behavior than about
loving behavior. As children we used our parents, teachers, relatives,
siblings, or characters in books, on TV, or in the movies to help us

discover how to be in the world. We emulated their manners, phi-losophies, and behaviors. They defined for us ways of being that we decided were right.

The young child's developing Inner Adult learns from the adults around it what being an Adult means. If the adults are abusive to themselves and others, children learn to abuse themselves and others. Only if the adults are loving to themselves and to their children, only if they are learning from their own Inner Child and from others, will the child have a role model for loving behavior.

We describe below some of the common unloving role models you may have experienced as a child. You may recognize yourself and oth-ers in any one of these models or in a combination of them. More than likely, you will see a combination of all of them in yourself. These role models correspond to the major ways the unloved, abandoned Child learns to protect itself.

The Compliant Model

This is the peace maker ("peace at any price"), the caretaker who believes that he or she is responsible for others' happiness and unhappiness. This person's whole sense of worth is tied up in pleasing others, believing that compliance will bring love and approval if he or she can only find the right way to please. Compliers and people-pleasers believe that giving up their own needs and adapting to the needs of others is the loving way to be, and that they do not have the *right* to make themselves happy, that making themselves happy is self-ish. Therefore, they need permission from someone else, usually their mate or children, to do what they want to do. Often, they do not even know what they want to do or what will make them happy, since they believe that all their happiness comes from pleasing others and getting approval. All conflicts are their fault, and they give in as a means to resolution.

Some women who assume this role view their subservient position as an appropriate one, believing that being subservient is in keeping with the laws of nature. These women may believe that men are stron-ger and wiser and that it is their duty to serve them well. They may also be characterized as martyrs who believe themselves to be all giving and all loving, even though inwardly resentful that they do not receive the accolades they believe they deserve. These women often get sick as the only way they know to take time for themselves and to say no to the demands of others.

Compliant women often attempt to define themselves through a man. Many men are only too happy to oblige them. A woman following this model will often become whoever her man wishes her to be. If he wishes her to be sexy and seductive, then that is what she is. If he wishes her to be quiet and demure or to act like a little girl, then that is what she does. If he wishes her to be less intelligent than he is, then that is how she behaves. If she still does not feel woman enough, she assumes she is not with the right man. Ultimately, she loses her entire identity, her entire sense of self. Her personal power is nonexistent. She has completely abandoned her Inner Child, and her abandoned Child tries to get love and approval by taking care of her husband's or lover's abandoned Child. This abandoned child is like an indentured servant, sold into servitude with no time or choice of its own.

Rachael was always a "good girl." As a child she had readily complied with her parents' demands and received conditional approval in return, which she interpreted as love. When she married Ron, she naturally continued to try to please him. She gave up her job as a legal secretary because her husband believed that a woman shouldn't work. Even though she really didn't enjoy it, she became adept at entertaining. She gave up most of her friends, because her husband believed they should do everything together and because he didn't like her single friends, fearing she would be influenced by them. She was always there when he came home from work (whether she wanted to be or not), because he hated coming into an empty house. She dutifully made love whenever he wanted, even when she wasn't interested in lovemaking. Over time she became less interested. After her children were born, she devoted herself entirely to them and was completely at their beck and call.

Rachael was a good girl, a good wife, a good mother, just as her mother had been. She never even asked herself if she was happy, or if other activities and people might excite her. She just did what she was "supposed" to do. She had an authoritarian Inner Adult who constantly told her that she was wrong and selfish if she wanted to do things for herself.

Men who adopt the compliant position are typical "nice guys," the passive men who seem nonexistent. These men are generally very quiet. They go to work—often becoming workaholics—and come home and watch TV or drink. They may leave childraising and decisionmaking to their wives. Children of these men often have no memory of their fathers. Or these men might be affectionate fathers but perceived by their children as weak, as always giving in to their wives.

If you adopted a compliant person as your role model, then your unloving Adult is probably primarily authoritarian, discounting your Inner Child's wants and needs. Your internal dialogue may go something like this:

"You don't count."

"You don't deserve to do what you want to do."

"What you want isn't important. What your husband/wife/children want is more important."

"Don't make trouble. Don't rock the boat. Just go along."

"It doesn't really matter. It's not important anyway."

"Don't hurt him/her; he/she can't take it."

"Just give in. It's easier than getting into an argument."

"Just lie, it's better than having him/her yell at you."

"You can't have what you want, so just go along."

"If you don't give in, you'll end up alone."

"It's okay to lose you, but don't lose him/her."

"Just do what's expected of you."

"You have to do what he/she wants or there'll be trouble!"

"You didn't do it right, again."

"You should be ashamed of yourself."

"You're selfish."

"Who do you think you are?"

"Work before play."

"You should . . ." "You shouldn't . . ." "You'd better . . ."

The Controlling Model

Controlling people believe they know the right way to be and do things and that it is their right to impose this on others.

The controlling woman is the classic "bitch," the hard, dominating, angry, critical housewife and mother. She rules the roost with an iron fist and everyone is afraid of her. She is generally married to a man who vacillates between compliance and resistance through indifference, giving in with some things but shutting down to her through alcohol, work, or TV. This woman believes that the way to get love and connection is by demanding it. She believes that she can change others' behavior by blaming them and convincing them that their behavior is wrong. She believes she can get people to do things her way by punishing them, which she does by being judgmental, cold, and sometimes even physically violent, especially with children. This woman is generally very righteous, believing that her way of doing things is *the* right way. She constantly complains that her husband (or her boyfriend or her children) bug her, neglect her, or don't care about her feelings. As with the compliant role model, she believes others are responsible for her happiness and unhappiness, but instead of trying to get love through compliance or seductiveness, she tries to control through intimidation. She is a master at creating fear and guilt in those around her and convincing them that her unhappiness is their fault.

Helen came into one of the women's groups because her life was feeling empty. She was a housewife with two small children, a life she had always wanted, yet things weren't turning out the way she had expected. Her husband no longer seemed interested in her and often didn't come home at night. When he was there, he rarely wanted to talk to her. When Helen talked she sounded like a machine gun. The words came out nonstop, with hardly a breath between sentences. She was constantly explaining herself, telling stories about how awful her husband was, and justifying her own behavior. If anyone tried to point out her own choices, she would just defend herself, explaining on and on how things couldn't possibly be her fault. Sometimes she would complain in an irritating, whining voice about something her husband had done. It did not take long for all of us to understand why this man didn't want to spend time with her.

Helen desperately wanted to connect with others, but because she believed that she was inadequate and unlovable, and that others were responsible for her feelings, she felt that the only way she could achieve the connection she wanted was to control others. And she believed she could control others with her machine-gun voice, her convincing, explaining, defending, and whining.

The man who takes the controlling position is experienced as unapproachable by his wife and children. They are afraid of him. His anger can easily erupt into rage when he doesn't get his way. Often he looks like a child having a temper tantrum, except that his tantrums can become physically violent. Such a man may also control others by being cold and judgmental. An icy look may be enough to get his way. He is generally married to a compliant woman.

Mike is a typical controlling man. He appears to be a very charming person, social and easy to talk to, a really nice man. This is his public image, but with his family, the niceness goes out the window the moment he is crossed. He becomes enraged the minute he doesn't get his way. He yells and may even become physically violent, but more often his anger is expressed through his eyes and his cold withdrawal of love. When he does express his anger outwardly, he appears to be totally out of control.

If you chose a controlling person as your primary role model, your inner dialogue from your authoritarian, judgmental, and critical Inner Adult might sound like this:

"Don't be so stupid."

"You're such a jerk."

"You'll never be good enough. You'll never do it right."

"You haven't got what it takes."

"What's the matter with you? What are you crying about? I'll give you something to cry about."

"You're ugly."

"Shut up. You don't know what you're talking about."

"You're crazy."

"You can't . . ." "You're not capable."

On the other hand, if you identified with a controlling parent, then your Inner Adult might be permissive, just leaving and letting your Inner Child rant and rave at others, in the same way your mother or father did, with no inner limits. The Inner Child, left in this position, generally has no respect for others' boundaries and will yell, hit, interrupt, snoop, and demand time, attention, affection, or sex. You might not be aware of any inner dialogue, which is the case when the Inner Adult abdicates responsibility and seems to disappear.

If you took a resistant position in reaction to a controlling parent, your inner dialogue might sound like this:

"Don't tell me what to do."

"I don't have to."

"You can't make me."

"Do it yourself."

"I can't."

This reaction might occur when someone else wants you to do something, or it might occur when your Inner Child wants something from you or wants you to do something. In this case, your Inner Adult is being permissive by neglecting the Inner Child's wants and needs.

The Resistant Model

Resistant people avoid responsibility through procrastination, incompetence, indifference, or forgetting. They often also deny the fact that their resistance is serving a purpose. They are rigid and defensive about their position, protesting that they are trying, yet they never seem to accomplish anything. They often appear lazy and mentally absent. They may escape with the help of alcohol, drugs, or TV, but deny that they have a problem.

Harold is a typical resistant man. His father was very handy around the house, and his controlling mother tried to force him to participate in his father's projects, so he learned to be extremely incompetent around the house. As an adult, he prefers to let his wife and children fix things. He has a hard time earning a living, even though sometimes he appears to try hard. There is always some reason why he isn't succeeding, some reason why he always has to rely on his wife to take care of him. When she gets exasperated with his laziness, he gets hurt and angry, accusing her of not trusting him. When she asks him to do anything around the house, he says he will and then doesn't. If she keeps at him, he gets mad at her for bugging him. He smokes a lot of marijuana and occasionally gets drunk, but denies that any of this is a problem. He is self-indulgent and self-centered, believing others should take care of him. His wife is a caretaker who becomes controlling when she gets frustrated.

If you had a resistant person as your role model, you might find that you have little inner dialogue and feel a kind of deadness inside. This is because you are resisting the wants, needs, and feelings of your Inner Child. You are dealing with your Child by being permissive, by going numb and ignoring it. At other times, when you find yourself procrastinating, the inner dialogue might sound like this:

"Why bother?"

"Who cares?"

"If you wait long enough, someone else will do it for you."

"I don't want to go to work. Let's just go back to sleep."

On the other hand, you might have reacted to an irresponsible, self-indulgent parent by becoming very responsible yourself. In this case, your inner dialogue might be the self-blaming dialogue of the compliant person.

None of the models described offer their real-life children adequate loving behavior because they do not know how to love themselves. They have all chosen to protect themselves and are operating as an unloving Adult and an abandoned Child, thus teaching their children to do the same.

The Loving Inner Adult

If your Inner Child felt free to tell you exactly what it wants from you, it would probably say something like this: "I want you to pay attention to me and to spend time with me. I want you to *listen to me* and really hear me when I'm trying to tell you something. I want you to know me, to know who I *really* am, not who you *think* I am. I don't want you to control me with 'shoulds' and rules, but I don't want you to indulge me either. I want you to consider what I want rather than just making up your mind by yourself without me. I want you to trust my instincts and intuition. I want you to always tell me the truth. I don't like it when you lie to me, like telling me I'm bad or that I can control people or that I'm responsible for others' feelings or that I'm selfish when I take care of myself. I feel confused when you lie to me. When you talk to me, don't lecture to me or talk *at* me. I want you to talk *to* me. I want you to protect me from other people's anger by taking over when others are acting from their ego. I want you never to shame me. I want you to know that I always have good reasons for what I want and feel, and I want you to want to know about my reasons rather than to blame and shame me. I want you to give me enough time to play, and I want you to take enough time to earn money for us so that I feel safe and taken care of. I want you to let me eat what I want as long as it's healthy. I want you to help me protect our body by not letting me put things into me that are not good for me. Whenever I'm upset, hurt, angry, or lonely I want you to spend time with me, learning about what I feel and why I feel that way. I want you to let me do the things that are really fun for me and make me feel alive. I want you to find friends for me who are loving and not to make plans for me with people with whom I am uncomfortable. I want you to protect me from being used and abused in any way. I want you to act in my behalf, making sure that I am safe and that my wants and needs are met. I want you to help me heal my pain by helping me replace my false beliefs with the truth and to provide loving people to help me with this. I want you to be a loving teacher with me. I want you to be nurturing, compassionate, soft, and gentle with me and to see all that I am. I want to feel love coming from your heart and not just talk coming from your head. I want to know that you are always with me so that I don't feel alone inside."

Your Inner Child is asking for unconditional love, something most of us know nothing about.

Unconditional Love

Being an unconditionally loving Adult to our Inner Child means that we love *without conditions*. It means that our love is *dependable and consistent*, regardless of how our Inner Child feels or behaves, or what our Child needs or wants. Our Child can count on us to stay *open to learning and acting in its behalf* even when the Child is upset or angry or feels deep pain, or when the Child wants something that is in conflict with what the Adult wants. Just as external children would not feel loved if you fed them once or twice a week or only occasionally paid attention to their pain or rarely did fun things with them, so your Inner Child will not feel loved unless it can count on you to *always* be there.

When one thinks of unconditional love, images of flowing softness come to mind. The power to totally dedicate oneself to loving, especially in the face of fear, has the feeling of strength and beauty. Some people feel that unconditional love cannot exist, that it is an absolute that can never be achieved. We feel that it is a goal, one that you can choose as often as you wish.

Anyone who has experience with animals, especially dogs, has experienced unconditional love. It is easier for animals to love unconditionally because they lack defined egos. When you scold dogs for some transgression, they usually respond with sad eyes and total vulnerability. They allow you to see their pain and are totally open. Their energy and eyes seem to say, "I know you are angry, but I love you, and I'm sorry you are unhappy." This act is very endearing to us, and in return we love our animals for their ability to love us so deeply.

Dogs seldom snap back or try to protect themselves, except when they have been severely mistreated and are afraid.

As a mother gazes into the eyes of her newborn child for the first time, and holds the warmth and softness of its body to hers, she experiences a new depth of tenderness. Even if you have never held a baby you can probably recall a time when you held a puppy in your arms, or smelled fresh bread baking, or were swept away by the beauty of a soft spring shower. This is the feeling your Child has when it feels loved unconditionally.

We all have the power to choose loving behavior with our Inner Child whenever we want. In order to behave lovingly, we have to feel loving, which means that we are not judging or shaming our Child. We may believe that we love our Child, yet often we don't feel and behave in loving ways towards our Inner Child. It is not enough to talk about loving your Child. You have to feel it and act on it. Being unconditionally loving to your Inner Child means being *devoted* to the Child. When a person says they love their Inner Child, but they don't act in behalf of the Child's needs, then they aren't devoted to their Child. They still are not being loving—they want someone *else* to be devoted to their Child. A person can like their Inner Child but still not be devoted to it, and until they are devoted, they are not being unconditionally loving. When you are devoted to your Inner Child, you do not let it suffer. If your Child is unhappy, you rush in to learn about the unhappiness and about what would bring happiness. Ignoring your Inner Child and letting it suffer fear or pain, or waiting for someone else to fix it is very unloving. For example, if your Child says to you that it is frightened of earthquakes (this happens frequently in Los Angeles), and you just say to your Child, "Don't worry. I'll take care of you," your Child will not feel loved and safe. You would need to ask your Child what it needed to feel safe and loved, and act accordingly. In addition, you would need to act in your Child's behalf by making sure you have an earthquake kit with everything in it you would need in case of a severe earthquake, just as loving parents would for their external children. Saying loving things to your Inner Child is not enough—you must take responsibility for *acting* in a way that protects and meets the needs of your Inner Child.

It might help to imagine that you are walking through life hand in hand with your Child, or with your Child playing next to you or in your arms, just as you might with a real-life child. If that child became upset, what would you do? Would you ignore it? Would you get someone else to handle the problem? Would you yell and tell the child that if it doesn't stop crying you will give it something to cry about? Would you tell it how bad or wrong it is and that it should be ashamed of itself? Would you shove it into another room until it stopped fussing? A real child would not feel loved if you behaved in these ways nor will your Inner Child. It will feel loved only if you learn about it and understand its problems and then act to relieve its pain.

It is impossible to learn and love when we judge. It is actually easier to learn and to love than to judge, and far less painful, but in our left-brain society, we tend to see everything in terms of right and wrong. From the day we are born, we are taught to judge everything. Things do not simply exist, they are either good or bad, right or wrong. Once you judge something as wrong, you won't be open to learning about it, and that's the problem. Our judgments keep us from being aware of the feelings and beliefs of our Inner Child. We will not allow ourselves to be aware of something we judge to be wrong or bad. When we are ashamed of our thoughts, feelings, and beliefs, we rob ourselves of an opportunity to find out who we are, what we are really like. The ego already believes we are basically bad, so it judges our thoughts and feelings as bad. But your Higher Self knows that you are a learning and growing human being and that, as such, you will be afraid sometimes, or brilliant and boring, or passionate and aloof, or accepting and arrogant, and everything else. You are all that you feel, and all that you feel is *acceptable*. When you can allow your Child to just *be—that* is unconditional love. There will be times when your Child is hurt or angry. Can you love it anyway? You can if you wish to learn about those feelings. You do not have to blame or shame yourself for having an ego; nor do you have to try to get rid of it. That only leads to further conflict within yourself. To love your Child unconditionally means that you accept your ego—your unloving Adult and your unloved Child. It is only your ego that shames itself. Your Higher Self never shames.

Protecting ourselves from learning about our fears is one of the things that gets in the way of loving our Inner Child. It is not the fears that cause the problem, but the choice to protect ourselves against them. The more we confront our fears and deal with them *in the moment*, the easier it becomes to be loving in every interaction. For example, you may be engaged in a lively conversation. You feel loving and are in tune with the other person. The next moment he or she says something that is painful or frightening to your Child. Now you have a choice. Do you disconnect from your Child, or do you choose to learn with and from your Child's feelings? The more times we can react with unconditional love toward our Child, the better we will feel about ourselves and the more we can love. The more we love, the happier we are.

Being unconditionally loving to our Inner Child means that we learn how to truly nurture our Child. One way the loving Adult nurtures the Child is by telling the Child the truth. Because *truth is love*, the truth is always nurturing, even if it is difficult to hear. It is far more loving to tell an Inner Child who was abused as a child that it was never truly loved by its parents than to continue to lie and make excuses for the unloving behavior of the parents. And then it is nurturing to allow the Inner Child to grieve the past. The Inner Child may need lots of time to move through old pain and grief; a nurturing loving Adult gives the Child this time.

As we said earlier, the hardest feeling to bear is aloneness. All of us felt this to one degree or another when we were children, and it is the feeling we most strongly protect ourselves against. It's a very frightening feeling, because as infants we could have died if we were left alone long enough, so the feeling of aloneness can make us feel like we're going to die. It taps feelings of powerlessness, of being unable to control our own lives, and unable to control others whose support we believe we need. But as long as we are afraid of this feeling, then we will always protect ourselves against it. Healing occurs when the loving Adult acknowledges these feelings within the Inner Child. It is the job of the Adult to witness these feelings and understand the cause of them, and enable the Child to experience them safely and move through them. This means providing the Child with both internal and external love, love from a friend or therapist who can hold you while your Child goes through the pain. Being there for the Inner Child's aloneness, not trying to take away the pain, but providing a loving arena to learn and heal, is one of the primary jobs of the loving Adult.

The loving Adult reflects to the Inner Child the Child's true identity, so the Child can replace his or her false beliefs with the truth. The following is an example of one of our clients talking to her Inner Child and telling her who she is.

You like to run and play, and you like to jump up and down and throw balls and laugh and shout and scream and make noise and slide down bannisters and jump from the top of the wardrobe onto the bed. And do jigsaw puzzles and play with the cat and love the dog and ride a bicycle. And you love to be happy, and you love to be joyful and smile and laugh and joke and be impish.

You're a very deeply caring, very sensitive little girl. You pick up on things really quickly. You can tell if somebody's sad, and you can tell if somebody's happy, and you can join in that with them. And you're friendly.

I know that when I'm there for you, you're really in tune with things and you're very intuitive. You seem to be able to sense things really quickly and clearly too. You see things sometimes that other people don't see. And you're good at wanting to tell the truth, too. You like to be honest with yourself and with other people, and I know that you really try to do that.

You can write lots of beautiful poetry. You have great feeling for things, although sometimes you find it hard to express what you feel. You're very passionate. You like to get involved with things and get carried away with them and forget about time. And you're good at learning, too. You remember things that are important to you, and you don't bother to remember the other things. I never used to think this, but now I think you're pretty smart and pretty intelligent, and you've gone to school and done all your assignments and you've gotten really good grades for them. And you're a good writer. Sometimes it's not easy to write, I know, but when you write it turns out pretty good—especially the poetry.

You're very good at music, at picking up an instrument and learning to play it—the guitar, flute, saxophone, keyboard—you can play them all. You seem to be able to pick something up and play around with it for a little while and, hey, you can do it! You just have a knack for playing music.

You're good at going out and climbing rocks and skiing and riding bicycles and, hey, you can juggle too. And you managed to go out and learn how to sail, single hand and skipper, and night sail and navigate, and you managed to sail that little laser all by yourself. And you learned to scuba dive. You're really very competent. There's lots of things you can do. Lots and lots. Lots of outdoor things, lots of things with nature.

I used to think you were the most ornery little kid around. I used to think you were horrible. I used to think you were mean and nasty for shouting and screaming and yelling and kicking and punching the whole time. And now, I know that you did that because you were hurting a lot. But underneath all that fear and anger and pain, there's somebody who's so sensitive and caring, and so gentle and warm and compassionate, and so capable, and so alive and energetic and enthusiastic that it would be difficult to know why anybody wouldn't like you. There's so many things that you can do and so much that you know.

It's sad that all those wonderful qualities have always been in there but were never able to come out until now. It's sad that they were covered up by aggression and anger. Because underneath, there's just so much softness and gentleness and love. And that's what's really real. That's who you really are. When I know you like this, I know you're really special.

Below is a summary of the basic behaviors necessary for loving re-parenting of your Inner Child.

1. Choose to learn about your Child's feelings and take responsibility for healing the fear and pain and creating joy.

2. Explore all painful or negative feelings, discover the false beliefs behind the pain, and teach the truth.

3. Never judge or shame the anger, fear, pain, excitement, passion, or achievements of your Child, or tell your Child she or he must "do it right." Accept that your Child always has important reasons for its feelings and behavior.

4. Act in your Child's behalf to eliminate present painful situations and create joy. Any action, even a wrong action, still has more progress and meaning in it than no action.

5. Be consistent and dependable in tuning into your Child daily and *acting* in behalf of its needs, wants, and desires without indulging or discounting them. The Adult and Child need to have an *equal voice* concerning needs, wants, and desires.

6. Courageously acknowledge and witness your Inner Child's deepest feelings of aloneness and loneliness. Be present with your love and compassion while your Child experiences these painful feelings from the past and present, and provide loving people to help your Child move through these feelings.

7. Reflect to your Child who he or she really is.

There are many things you can do to understand what it means to love your Inner Child. One of the best things is to read good books on child rearing, applying them to yourself instead of to an external child (see Suggested Reading). Another is to look for other people to use as role models, watching how they treat themselves, their children, and you. Erika describes below how Margie modeled unconditional love for her.

One day Margie came to my house to work on the book with me. I had had a terrible week, and when she arrived I was anything but loving. I became a victim the moment she walked through the door and started blaming her and the rest of the world for everything I was ever unhappy about! I was totally in my ego. Although I could see in Margie's eyes the pain my behavior caused, I seemed locked into my choice and wasn't about to abandon it; it kept me protected from the aloneness I was really feeling at the time. As I continued this weary monologue, I felt her move around the room with me. Then she said lovingly, "Erika, I see you really need to be angry right now and it's okay. I am here for you." I felt her unconditional love. She was in pain from being blamed and decided to love anyway. I was so very moved and safe with her that it allowed me to open to my real pain and then move through it. It took me only a few moments to get at the real pain. She held me in her arms while I cried and took responsibility for what hurt me and for my actions.

In those first moments, she made the decision to see me as a person in pain rather than taking my attack personally. She was very aware of her own pain and felt it deeply, but chose to love me anyway, and so she was open and soft and stayed in her Higher Self. Even now, when I encounter someone in pain and they attack me personally, I remember Margie's softness and the lesson I learned about choice. Sometimes I respond with unconditional love, but sometimes I don't. If I don't, I just learn about how my ego got in my way that time, and maybe the next time I will achieve my goal. Experiencing how she was loving to me helped me learn to be loving to my own Inner Child.

Below is a brief essay written by Rosey, one of our clients, about how she awakened her nurturing Inner Adult.

It has taken a long time for me to understand that I have been a scared Child trying to function in an adult world without a loving Inner Parent to help me. It has taken me even longer to make the decision to develop that nurturing, caring part of myself, and to be responsible for my own happiness and my own experience in the world. I had not wanted to assume that position until I was almost thirty-three years old.

It's not that I'm stupid or even just slow—far from it. I really had thought I was a responsible and mature person. At some level though, I had always known that I was different from most other people I knew. The difference that I have come to discover for myself is that I abandoned myself so completely at such an early age that my internal Adult never even started to function. My parents showed me how to pretend that I had my own internal Adult, and I learned their behavior, but I never learned the internal connection with my Child that would have transformed those years from empty to fulfilled and satisfying.

I didn't want to know that all the tasks I had been trying all my life to get others to do for me in the arena of personal responsibility were really my own work to do. I didn't want to know that only I could make myself truly happy or truly miserable. I didn't want to know that I had abandoned my Inner Child emotionally and physically abused her.

When the time arrived to start seeing things as they really were, the decision to be my own loving, caring, nurturing Adult was a very simple one. The challenge since then has been to recognize that in every single moment of the day, I can choose to love myself or hate myself, and that if I am not actively loving myself in some way, then I am neglecting and therefore abusing myself. It's really as simple as that. I believe that when I have practiced loving myself enough in a certain way, I will automatically internalize those loving messages and I will then be able to focus on another aspect of self-neglect. In this way, piece by piece, I believe that I can re-parent myself and that I will gradually come to know myself.

People who have their own internal self-connection have a distinct advantage in their everyday lives. They feel self-assured. They are soft but not weak, strong but not aggressive, powerful but not forceful. They have self-respect and self-awareness—they really know themselves. They have strong views and opinions but don't need to defend them to others. They don't feel personally attacked by someone else's misplaced aggression. They know they deserve love and affection and are equally capable of giving and receiving both. They are in touch with the seriousness of life as well as the joy and happiness. They are curious and outgoing, unafraid to learn something new. They are creative and spontaneous, they make things happen for themselves rather than being at the mercy of other people and events. They have learned to take care of themselves and are not afraid of the responsibility that goes with that task. Many of them are not even aware that they have this internal connection because it has always been so natural for them—they never abandoned themselves.

The more a person connects internally, loving Adult to loving Child, the more fulfilled his or her life will be. This internal connection and love is the key that unlocks the door to our deepest questions and answers. It is the base on which to build our lives as loving human beings. When we love ourselves, we can love others; when we hate ourselves we ultimately hate others.

When you learn to love your Inner Child, then the fear, pain, and aloneness of the abandoned Child gradually heals and you experience the joy, passion, and vitality of your loved Child, and create the love, power, and compassion of your Higher Self. Learning to lovingly reparent your Inner Child is the key to all of this.

The best way to become unconditionally loving to your Inner Child is to practice. As with any new skill, loving takes practice. We have been practicing being unloving to our Child our whole lives, and we are very good at it. Becoming loving to your Child is not something you can do in your head, it is something you have to actually *do*. The next section offers processes to help you practice connecting to your Child in a loving way.

Part 2

PROCESSES

CHAPTER 8

Processes for Yourself

It is important to note that the need to find the Inner Child is part
of every human being's journey toward wholeness.
Healing the Shame that Binds You
JOHN BRADSHAW

When you are first learning to connect to your Inner Child, the practice
must be done in writing or out loud. If you try to do it in your head,
you will find yourself getting lost and not being able to distinguish
between the different voices.

You need to learn to distinguish between four different internal
voices: the loving Adult, the unloving Adult, the loved Child, and the
abandoned Child. The voices that have been operating in your head
most of your life are the unloving Adult and the abandoned Child, the
two voices of your ego. Since we have been practicing these ego voices
for so long, silent dialogue between the loving Adult and the loved
Inner Child generally disintegrates into the ego's voices without our
even recognizing it. It is only when we hear ourselves out loud or put
the dialogue in writing that we learn to tell the difference.

As with any skill that you want to practice, you must be willing to
set aside definite times to do it. You must schedule it into your day just
as you schedule in time to work, eat, sleep, or spend with others. We
have found that it works well to schedule fifteen minutes in the morn-
ing and fifteen minutes in the evening. In addition, you must be willing
to find time during the day to talk with your Child when it feels tense,
anxious, scared, sad, or angry. If you are not used to paying attention
to your solar plexus, to "focusing" (see *Focusing* by Eugene Gendlin)
inward, you might not even be aware of these feelings. Part of the
practice is learning to pay attention to your feelings. You can't learn
from your feelings if you don't know that you are feeling something.

When you first start to talk with your Child, it is easy to slip into the
unloving Adult without realizing it. Your first challenge, then, in the
process of healing and creating inner connection is to learn to be a

loving Adult to your Inner Child. Your Child cannot heal until you know how to love it.

Much of what you hear at first from the Child is the voice of the wounded, abandoned Child, the part of you that feels so alone and is terrified of that feeling. It is very important to realize that *this is not who your Child really is*. This is your Child filled with painful experiences and false beliefs, and with the fear, anger, shame, guilt, and grief that come from these experiences and beliefs. When you are further along in your learning process and are connecting with your loved Inner Child, you will often hear very wise answers to your questions, but at the beginning much of what you hear from your Child is its fear, anger, grief, and pain. You may spend many months of being present for your abandoned Child in a loving way before some of the inner pain begins to heal and some of the anger at childhood caregivers (and at you for abandoning it) begins to melt away. Your Child may have much pain and anger from having been rejected, abandoned, controlled, and engulfed by parents and others. You need to hear and experience in a loving way whatever memories and feelings your Child is ready to offer you. You will find that when your Child truly trusts you, clear memories from childhood will begin to emerge. We have worked with many people who, having been blocked for years with no childhood memories, suddenly find memories coming up within a few months of beginning this work with their Child. This occurs, however, only if they are consistent and loving in the dialogue with their Child.

Your Inner Child needs to learn that it can depend on you. If you commit to talking with your Child every day, but you don't follow through on your commitment, your Inner Child feels disappointed and hurt. If this happens often enough, your Child may stop speaking to you for awhile, until it feels it can trust you not to abandon it again. Your Child may not even start to speak to you until it believes that you will show up every day. Shawn, a client of ours, told us that he wrote to his Child every day for three weeks before his Child answered back. He didn't quite believe he had an Inner Child but decided to persist anyway. Once his Child started speaking, volumes came out, but whenever Shawn didn't write for a few days, his Child would withdraw and not speak to him for a day or two.

When you are asking questions or speaking from your Adult, tune into your thoughts and your caring feelings by focusing your attention in your head and heart. When you are speaking from your Child, tune into your feelings by focusing in the area above your navel and below your rib cage. That is your solar plexus, or third chakra. Ask yourself how old your Inner Child is. Most people feel that their Child is around five or six, but he or she can be younger or older. Find a picture of yourself at that age and spend some time seeing who this Child really is.

There are two conditions necessary for learning from your Child. First, you must believe that your Child has important and valid reasons for feeling and behaving as it does. If you are judging your Child's feelings and behavior as good or bad, right or wrong, then your Child may be afraid to talk to you, afraid that you will judge it for its feelings. Your Child will feel loved and safe only when you believe it has good reasons for whatever it wants, needs, and feels. Second, you must be open to experiencing your Child's pain. If you are afraid of pain and unwilling to experience it, then you will protect yourself against feeling it and taking responsibility for it.

The dialogue begins with the Adult asking the Child questions or making statements with the intent to learn about and understand the Child's wants, needs, and feelings. The Adult is open, curious, caring, and nonjudgmental, knowing that the Child has very good reasons for its feelings and wanting to learn about the beliefs behind any negative or painful feelings. If there is no true intent to learn, then the Inner Child will feel that the Adult is just interrogating and controlling it. Without a true intent to learn no real connection is possible. You cannot fake an intent to learn. Your Inner Child knows when you are truly open, caring, and interested, or when you are just performing an exercise and acting open.

The loving Adult can ask questions or make statements such as:

"What are you feeling?"

"What do you want or need right now?"

"I know you're angry and I'd like to hear your anger."

"Are you angry with me? It's okay to yell at me."

"Are you in pain right now? Can you tell me what it's about?"

"It's okay to cry. I'm here for you."

"I know you're feeling anxious. What is your anxiety about?"

"How do you feel about_____?" (Name a person)

"How do you feel about the work we do?"

"I'd like to understand why you feel scared of_____."

"I'd like to understand why you don't like_____."

"Tell me more about that."

Throughout the day, whenever you become aware of feeling anxious, depressed, scared, tense, angry, dead, uncomfortable, hurt, or sad, you can ask your Inner Child questions such as:

"What's causing these feelings?"

"How can I help you with these feelings?"

"What do you need from me?"

"Am I letting you down or not taking care of you in some way? How?"

"Have I been ignoring you? Discounting you? Controlling you? Judging you?"

Sometimes present situations—people and events—can touch off past experiences and create feelings of anxiety, anger, pain, and fear. When you become aware of feeling these feelings, you can ask:

"Is something happening now that reminds you of something that happened when we were little?"

"Does this person remind you of mom, dad, a brother or sister, a grandparent?"

"Does this situation remind you of a traumatic experience that we had when we were little?"

"I really want to know about everything you remember from the past. Your memories are very important to me and I want to help you heal old fears and pain."

"Do you need me to provide us with someone to help with this? Do you need to be held while you go through this pain?"

At times during the dialogue the loving Adult may need to affirm how he or she feels about the Child:

"I'm here for you. I'm not going away again."

"I love you and your happiness is the most important thing in the world to me."

"You are so smart. Thank you for all this wonderful wisdom."

"Your creativity amazes me."

"It's truly okay for you to feel this anger, even if it's at me. I won't stop loving you no matter how angry you feel."

"You can keep crying as long as you need to. You are not alone. I'm here for you."

"It's okay to make mistakes. You are lovable even if you make mistakes."

"You don't have to do it 'right.' I will continue to love you no matter what you say, even if you say nothing at all."

The dialogue process can also help you become aware of what you want in everyday situations. You can facilitate this by asking your Child questions such as:

"What are your favorite foods?"

"What would you like for dinner tonight?"

"What do you feel like wearing today?"

"What are your favorite colors?"

"Who do you like to spend time with?"

"What would you like to do this Sunday?"

"What were your favorite activities when you were little?"

"What kind of books do you like to read?"

"What kind of music do you like?"

"What kind of movies do you like?"

"What kinds of vacations do you like?"

"What kind of exercise do you like?"

"What kinds of creative things do you like to do? Art? Crafts? Music? Writing?"

"What are some of the things you've always wanted to do but have never done? Learn to fly? Learn to sail? Learn karate?"

Sometimes your Adult and your Child have different tastes in movies, music, books, or vacations. When this is the case, it's important to find a way to meet the needs of both aspects of your personality.

When your Child answers your questions, the Adult you needs to respond by active listening, by asking another question to clarify, by making a loving statement, or by offering the truth. Active listening is a skill that has to be practiced. The term was coined by Thomas Gordon in *Parent Effectiveness Training*, and means listening with your heart and feeding back what you hear to let your Child know you really understand. For example, if your Child says, "You don't love me. You never listen to me or spend time with me or do what I want," and you respond with "Well, I'll try harder," your Child may not feel heard. If you actively listen and respond with "Sounds like you're feeling sad and angry at me because I'm not taking good care of you," your Child will feel heard and understood.

The reason it's so important to practice loving dialogue in writing and out loud is because it takes much practice to shift from our habitual unloving inner dialogue to loving inner dialogue. Most people are not aware of how much they judge, control, ignore, and discount their Inner Child—they just do it automatically. It takes practice to change that. The goal is to have consistently loving inner dialogue. This means not only practicing the written and oral dialogue, but consciously shifting the tone of our dialogue throughout the day from unloving to loving. For example, if you're an artist and you do a painting you particularly like, an unloving dialogue might begin: "Yeah, it's good, but it's just a fluke," while a loving dialogue might begin: "Thanks for your creativity. I really appreciate your wonderful ideas." With any behavior, skill, or talent, you can denigrate yourself ("That was okay but it wasn't perfect") or you can appreciate yourself ("Hey! That was great! You really did a good job!" or "That's okay, you're still learning. You're doing just fine. It's okay not to be perfect. I appreciate your effort, your willingness to try").

Since many of us were demeaned, ignored, ridiculed, judged, laughed at, or discounted as children by our parents and other caregivers, we learned to do that to ourselves. By continuing to do that to ourselves, we perpetuate our low self-esteem through our unloving inner parenting. *Re-parenting ourselves means giving ourselves the love and approval we never received from others.*

The more you practice loving dialogue with your Inner Child, the easier it will be for you to know what to ask and how to respond. Some of the books in the Suggested Reading section are very helpful in teaching you how to ask questions and respond so that you can learn from your Child. When you are answering as the Child, allow yourself to feel like a little child. Put your attention into your gut, allowing yourself to move out of your head and into your feelings, and answer with whatever emerges. You cannot *figure out* what your Child feels—you have to allow the feelings to emerge.

Writing

Writing is a powerful way to connect with your Inner Child. Because the dialogue is down on paper, you can easily go back and learn about the different voices that may have participated. Some people write their Adult questions with their dominant hand and write their Child's answers with their nondominant hand. If you are right-handed, then you would write your Child's responses with your left hand.

If you have never held such a dialogue, you might want to start by writing a letter explaining the process and telling your Child how you feel about him or her, even if what you feel is negative. For example, you might say "I'm not even sure you exist but I'm willing to give it a try," or "I'm really afraid of you. I think you're the one who has always gotten me into trouble." In addition, it can be helpful to let your Child write a letter to you. Below is a letter written to Sue from her Child during a workshop. The letter is written in the nondominant hand and is the first communication Sue ever had from her Child. It let her know that her Child really exists.

Dear Mommy,

I need you I miss you I wish you would come home I am so lonely. I am not having any fun here There are no friends, no one to talk to I want to be with you. To feel your arms around me, to know that you care. Please notice me I want your love — don't leave me.

Love,

Susie

Below is an example of written dialogue between tall, dark-haired Janet, a client of ours in her mid-thirties, and her Inner Child. When Janet first started writing, her Child wouldn't speak to her. Then Janet discovered that she was unconsciously telling her Child that she was not available to hear her anger. Once she made the decision to hear the anger, her Child opened up to her.

Adult: How do you feel about Dad?

Child: That fucking bastard. I hate his guts—keep him away from me. Tell him to fuck off and leave me alone. Tell him to piss on himself. I hate him. Is that clear enough for you? Now you fuck off and don't ask me such stupid questions. Stupid bitch. You're a real fucking jerk too. Miss almighty. Miss supreme. Who the hell do you think you are? What makes you so special? Fuck off. Keep away from me. Don't talk to me. Don't come near me.

Adult: That's a really loud and clear message. I hear your hatred and anger, but I don't know what they're about. Can you tell me? (Active listens and then asks question to clarify.)

Child: Are you fucking stupid or what? Didn't I make it clear? I don't want you around me. I don't want you near me. I don't want you to speak to me. What's it going to take to get through to you? Piss off.

Adult: No, I won't. You've always done this, since you were very small. You've always pushed people away when you were hurting. You've never let anyone get close enough to love you and care for you. I'm not going to keep on doing the same thing anymore. I'm not going to be pushed away by you. I see you hurting unbearably and then disguising the pain with anger and rage at me and everyone else. I know you're hurting under there, and I'm not going to abandon you any more to deal with it alone. We have to start dealing with this together. I'm here for keeps. What is it that you really want when you're so busy pushing people away and yelling at them? What do you really want them to do? (Makes a loving statement and asks another question.)

Child: I want them to make me feel better because it hurts so much. But I know they can't make me feel better. They'll just make it worse, so I'd rather deal with it myself. I don't want anyone to know how much I really hurt. I don't want them to think I can't deal with it by myself. I don't want them to think I'm weak and defenseless. I'm strong and I can take care of myself, and nobody's going to hurt me. I won't let them hurt me. I won't let them close enough to hurt me. They can't get close to me when I yell and kick and scream and push them away. So tell everyone to keep away from me. I won't let anyone in. I won't let anyone close enough to hurt me.

Adult: I know you were really afraid of people in the family hurting you, and I can see and understand why. They didn't know how to care for you and you were often hurt by their actions (active listens). But that situation has changed now. You're no longer with those same people in that house. [Janet's Child is coming from false beliefs from childhood, so here Janet is offering her Child the truth.] The people around you now won't treat you the same way, and if they tried to, I'm here now and I can protect you. And besides, I'm the one you can turn to for help. I wasn't here before, but I am now. You couldn't have asked me for help before, but you can now. I'm here to care for you and help you and love you and protect you. You can turn to me instead of being angry and hard outside. (Janet makes a loving statement.)

Child: That's right. You weren't here for me. You've never been here for me. You left me and I've been feeling pretty stupid ever since—making a fool of myself, because you weren't here when you were supposed to be. Fucking stupid jerk. Do you know what it's been like to struggle the way I have? I've had to deal with everything by myself with no help from you. I hate you. You're so fucking stupid and lazy. Don't start thinking you're going to get me to change my mind about you either. You're not going to fool me or trick me. I won't let you get away with that. You can just stay right where you are. You may think you've got plans and you're going to do things but I've got news for you. You can't do anything without my help and I'm not going to let you off that easily. You have to make everything up to me. Before, you left me to deal with things alone and now I'm going to get back at you. You'll just have to wait for me, wait until I'm ready. Or we won't do anything. I'll punish you. I hate you.

This dialogue session ended here. The next day Janet and her Child had another session. She was aware that her Child was going through a lot of pain.

Adult: I can hear and see and feel that you're in a great deal of pain right now. The pain seems completely overwhelming to you. I'm sorry you feel so much pain and sorrow, and I'm glad you are able to let me in it and share it with me. I know you have always had to struggle through times like these alone in the past. I know it has sometimes felt unbearable to you. I see how deeply hurt you are and I care about you very much. I see a small child, miserable, and unbearably alone, afraid of anyone coming close, afraid of accepting help from others. Afraid to be herself. There's so much hurt under the tough exterior. So much aloneness, such a fragile child trying to bear the weight of a mountain of pain and anger and hurt and disappointment. It's okay to feel the pain. It's okay to do it now.

Child: I feel like you've let me down forever. I want you and need you to be here for me now. I have to have your total involvement and commitment. It has to be real. I don't want to have to go on fighting and yelling and screaming. I want to feel safe to be soft and natural and gentle and real and whole.

Adult: You are so beautiful. You don't have to go on fighting anymore. I won't let anyone attack you. I won't let anyone hurt you. I won't hurt you.

The next day she had the following dialogue:

Adult: I never realized until maybe yesterday and today how deep and intense some of your feelings are. I realized you felt like killing George [her brother] and Dad—just for starters. Those are very strong feelings of hatred and rage and anger, and I know they disguise a lot of hurt in you too.

Child: Yes, I do want to kill George, little fuckhead. He used me and stole from me and I hate him. I don't want him in my life, and I want him to give back the money that he took. I'd like to kill him. And my Dad's a piece of shit. He never cared for me and doesn't care about me to this day. He's not interested in me, he's just relieved that he doesn't have to take care of me, doesn't have to do things for me. They're both shitheads. I hate them both.

Adult: It's okay to hate them. It's okay to feel mad and angry and want to kill them. I'm sorry I wasn't around to help you when things were tough for you. I'm sorry I gave all that money to George. I'm sorry I abandoned you, and I'm sorry you hurt so much. If you want to stop carrying the world on your shoulders, you can drop the weight any time you feel like it. I'll be here to help you find a new way, one that helps you to feel good. I won't go away. I'll stay with you. I want you to be able to get through this and enjoy life more. I'll walk with you, hand in hand, through the pain and anger and disappointment. I wish it could be easier for you. I know you feel overwhelmed by all your intense emotions, and so you cut them off. It doesn't have to be like that any more. You can start to feel them gradually and gently and build up to the most intense. It won't take long once you start to let it out.

If you're angry at me, you can tell me that too. I know I've let you down over and over again. I'm sorry I did that. I'm sorry I hurt you and abandoned you and didn't help you. You deserved better than I gave you. You deserve my love and affection and caring, all the time. I wish I had been able to give them to you. I wish I had decided earlier to take that responsibility. I'm sorry I let the abuse go on for so long. I'm sorry I abused you. I wish I'd never left you alone for one single second. I wish I'd always been present for you and connected to you. I know you're hurting as a result of my leaving you and abusing you. I'm sorry.

Child: I feel really sad and hurt that I wasn't good enough for you and that you didn't like me enough to be around for me. I wanted you to help me. I wanted your companionship and friendship and caring and support, but I never got it. You always left, and I've felt so hated by you, so disliked, so unworthy and bad. What could I possibly have done that you hated me so much that you didn't speak to me for years and years, and never told me you loved me? What could possibly have been so horrible about me that you chose to ignore me and criticize me and judge me and shout at me for so long? Why didn't you ever tell me you loved me and cared for me? Why haven't you ever properly taken care of me? Why did you leave? Where did you go? What could possibly have been so important to you that you haven't wanted to know me?

Adult: You never did anything, ever, that caused me to hate you or dislike you. I just never decided to be responsible for you. There's nothing wrong with you and there never has been [again, telling the Child the truth]. I just didn't show up before. I got frightened very early on, and I was too scared to show up afterwards. There's nothing the matter with you. You're beautiful and I love you. I never bothered to recognize your existence before. I chose to ignore you. I know that I hurt you, and I'm deeply sorry. I hope I can make it up to you from now on. You deserve nothing but my love and caring. You deserve the best from me and I'm going to give you the best I know how. I want to learn from you and with you. I will be here for you.

I feel tired. It's time for bed. Good night. I love you. You are very special to me and I will never abandon you again. Now I know you exist I will be here for you all the time. [Janet drew a little heart for her Child at the end of this dialogue.]

Below is a dialogue written by Melissa, a client of ours who has been a caretaker for her husband, Marvin, for many years and is now attempting to let go of the marriage. She has always experienced her husband as closed to learning, but she tends to keep trying to teach him to open up. She continues to hope that if she can just say the right thing, he will open up. Melissa has been working with her Inner Child for a few months and is at the point where her Child is offering her a great deal of wisdom.

Thursday, 10:00 P.M.

Adult: Why did we get sick?

Child: Not enough sleep and you making me take care of Marvin.

Adult: How can I help?

Child: *Let me speak when I don't like something!*

Friday, 3:00 A.M.

Adult: What are you feeling?

Child: Tired, and I can't sleep.

Adult: Why not?

Child: Too many thoughts going around in your head.

Adult: What has to happen to stop them?

Child: I guess we must be disconnected. Why don't you connect to me?

Adult: What do you need right now?

Child: I need you to tell me it's okay to be happy.

Adult: Of course it's okay. It's wonderful. There is nothing wonderful about suffering.

Child: But Marvin puts me down when I'm happy.

Adult: I know. But I'll take care of you when he does.

Child: What will you do?

Adult: I'll let you say "This doesn't feel good," and walk away.

Child: You've never done that. You always get into asking him why he's behaving the way he is, thinking that shows an intent to learn, but it's not. To learn means to tune in to me and act for me. Asking him why is trying to get him to be soft and open and is a manipulation. It's trying to get him to learn when he is closed. The only time to ask why is when he is already open.

Adult: Yes, I've done that a lot. So I have to accept his being closed and just walk away?

Child: Yeah, if you were to get how simple it is—just tune in to me and leave when I get tense. Then we could get rid of all this chatter, because there would be nothing to say.

Not only will it take time for the Child to open up, but it may take quite a bit of time and practice to learn to be a loving Adult. Going over your writing can help you to learn about how you are being unloving. In the following dialogue Roberto had just begun to write and was having a great deal of difficulty with it. He had been functioning as an abandoned Child his whole life with his Adult rarely making an appearance, either in work or in relationships. He is a recovering alcoholic and drug addict and has done much work in AA. Roberto, a physical therapist, recently broke his arm in a car accident and has not been able to work much.

Adult: What do you want?

Child: I want to be loved and cared for. I want you to take care of us.

Adult: I *want* to take care of us! [Roberto tends to say "I want to do this or that" and not do it. He is still not saying, "I will . . ."]

Child: Then *do* it, damn you! Nobody else will! [The Child is reacting to Roberto's habit of saying "I want to" and not following through.]

Adult: You hurt and I'm trying to take care of you. [Again, Roberto says "I'm trying" rather than "I will."]

Child: You're full of shit. You want to stay in self-pity and die. [The Child is not buying the "I'm trying."]

Adult: No more! I care and I love us and this dialogue is going to help us to heal. [Roberto is selling his Child rather than learning and asking his Child why he told him he was full of shit.]

Child: This dialogue is bullshit too! I'm scared.

Adult: This dialogue is going to help save our life. [Still selling, with no intent to learn about the Child's fear.]

Child: I need a nap.

Adult: Okay.

Roberto skipped writing the next day, Sunday, and wrote again on Monday.

Adult: I love you and I am committed to taking care of you and learning about and from you. How do you feel?

Child: I feel better, but I'm angry with you that you didn't write to me yesterday.

Adult: I felt good from church and I apologize! [Roberto is explaining and defending instead of learning about his Child's anger.]

Child: There seems to always be some excuse. [His Child is not buying the explanation.] Either you're too tired or in too much physical pain. We need so much time together! I'm scared now, and you haven't been able to take care of more business.

Adult: I think you are stealing my lines. Tell me about your fear. [Now he moves into an intent to learn.]

Child: I'm scared that we'll shut down and then we'll be on the streets and we won't come back. I'm lonely and I need some fun.

Adult: Okay, let's go for a walk! [Roberto moves away from learning and attempts to fix his Child rather than asking him what he wants.]

Child: First, I want to tell you how much I miss Patti! We had so much fun! I'm angry at you because you closed her away just like all the rest.

Adult: Patti was too young and not committed to her recovery. I'm sorry I picked wrong. [Roberto explains rather than attempts to understand his Child's feelings.]

Child: I'm scared about work. How are you going to feed us?

Adult: I'm trying as hard as I can. We have physical problems which must heal. [Roberto makes no attempt to learn about and understand his Child's feelings.]

The next day Roberto had this dialogue with his Child:

Adult: What's going on today?

Child: I feel bad! I hurt and I'm scared! Why aren't we working more?

Adult: Honey, we're working as hard as we're able. If we go too fast we'll jeopardize our arm. Didn't you enjoy the bicycle ride to the chiropractor's?

Child: Yes, that was fun. Thank you. I'm feeling sad. How long are we going to have all this physical pain and stress from not working?

Adult: I'm sorry you feel so sad today. Most of the pain we're experiencing is God's miracle of healing. [A Child is not helped by
this sort of metaphysical explanation. Again, there is no attempt to learn about his Child's sadness.]

Child: Fuck God, I'm sick and tired of hurting!

Roberto was unwilling to learn about his Child's feelings of anger
and sadness and ended the dialogue here. As long as Roberto maintains his intent to protect, no learning and healing can take place. His
Child does not feel loved by this dialogue.

Talking

Talking out loud with the Child is another very powerful way to
connect. For some people it works better than writing because it is
more immediate. You can't write as fast as you think, but you can talk
as fast as you think. And if you are angry or in pain, it may be more
releasing to do it out loud. Some people find access to their Inner
Child more easily when they talk out loud. For them, writing is too
intellectual.

In a spoken dialogue, it is helpful to use a picture of yourself as a
child and a picture of yourself as you are now. Set up two chairs and
put your Child's photo on one chair and your Adult's on the other.
When you are speaking as the Adult, speak to the picture of your
Child, and when you are speaking as the Child, speak to the picture of
your Adult. You may need to change chairs each time you change
voices, since it is easy to get confused between the voices. You proceed
in the same way you do in the writing—the Adult starts by asking a
question of the Child. When you are speaking as the Child, allow yourself to feel little and allow your voice to be a child's voice. If feelings
come up, allow your Child to cry or yell. When speaking as the Adult,
move into a calm, open mode, as you would with any five-year-old
child whom you truly want to know.

Many people find it helpful to use a large soft doll to represent their
Child. Speak to the doll when you are talking to your Child and hold
the doll against you with its face facing your Adult when you are
speaking as the Child. If you don't like dolls, a large cuddly stuffed
animal will do just as well.

Buy a doll or animal that you relate to from your Inner Child. Holding this doll or animal in times of stress can actually give your Inner
Child comfort. Some of our clients who have trouble remembering that

they have an Inner Child have found that carrying around their doll or animal reminds them to check in on how they are feeling and that they are responsible for their Inner Child.

Internal Dialogue

As we stated earlier, the goal is to have a constant loving flow between your Adult and your Child, between your thoughts and your feelings. We are in a place of wholeness whenever we achieve this balance. If you practice the written or verbal dialogue with your Child every day, you will find that gradually you are experiencing this loving inner connection between your Adult and your Child more and more of the time. *The only way for your internal dialogue to become loving instead of unloving is for you to practice every day.* As you become more proficient at being aware of your loving and your unloving thoughts and feelings, you will find yourself responding to situations in the moment, instead of an hour later or a day later. How often have you realized what you wished you'd said or done long after the fact? That's because you were not tuned in and connected in the moment: your loving Adult was not paying attention to the experience of your Child.

As you become conscious of the feelings of your Child, you will know immediately when your Child is upset. You will notice the tension or ache in your stomach, or in some other part of your body such as your legs or shoulders, the signal that something is amiss. Once your Child has learned to trust you, you can ask it then and there what is wrong, and you will immediately get an answer. Your Child may say to you, "This person is lying to you. I can feel it," or "This person is manipulating you," or "This person is closed, not open to learning," or "This doesn't feel good. Take me away," or "This situation is dangerous. Be careful."

You will also become more aware of what you want in any given moment. You'll know when you are hungry, what you feel like eating, when you feel full, when you want to go to sleep, what you really want to do in your free time, who you really want to spend time with, what colors you really like, or what kind of clothes you like. You will become guided more by your needs and wants and less by your "shoulds."

Exploring Fears and Beliefs

Most of our fears and the false beliefs that create them come from our childhood experiences. Our beliefs about not being able to handle our pain, about our worth, adequacy, and lovability, about being able to control how others treat us or feel about us, and about being able to control others (if only I'm open enough or loving enough, then he or she will be open too), our beliefs about being unable to make ourselves happy, about being responsible for another's feelings—these all come from childhood experiences. Even though these are all false beliefs, we adopted them for good reasons, and we probably will not be able to change the behavior that results from these beliefs until we understand where we got them and what purpose they serve. It is the job of the loving Adult to learn about the beliefs of the unloving Adult and the unloved Child—the beliefs of the ego. You can ask yourself questions such as:

"What is my belief about my ability to handle pain (or about my lovability, my ability to control others, my feeling responsible for others, others' responsibility for me, and so on)?"

"Where did I get this belief? What childhood experiences created this belief?"

"What do I gain by acting as if this belief were true?"

"What am I afraid of? What would happen if I stopped acting as if this belief were true?"

Sam, a client of ours, describes the process he went through in confronting some false beliefs.

I've been a caretaker my whole life. As a child I took responsibility for my mother's feelings, and as an adult I've taken responsibility for my wife's feelings. My caretaking took two distinct forms: giving in to others and teaching. I would go along with what my wife wanted to avoid her anger, and then I would point out to her the things she needed to deal with, the learning she needed to do. As I became aware of these things in therapy, I gradually stopped giving in, but I couldn't seem to stop teaching. It was like an obsession. I felt that if I could just point out the exact right thing to her, she would see what she was doing and stop being angry and disconnected from me. I saw that it wasn't working—in fact it was working against me, because she resisted anything I said. But I couldn't stop doing it; I was addicted to it.

Then I had a session where I contacted the deep feelings of loneliness in my Inner Child and I saw that I had spent my life caretaking and teaching to avoid these deeply painful feelings. I realized that I believed that I couldn't handle these feelings, and that caretaking and teaching would stop my wife from disconnecting from me so that I wouldn't have these feelings. Once I opened to the loneliness that my Inner Child feels when my wife disconnects, and once I realized that I could handle these feelings, the addiction to teaching disappeared completely. I saw that believing that I could keep her from disconnecting from me was a false belief, but that it had protected me all this time from feeling lonely.

Sam could not change his behavior, which was unloving to himself and to his wife, until he understood the good reasons—the fears and false beliefs—behind his behavior. When your Adult learns with your Inner Child, then the false beliefs of the ego can be uncovered and you can move toward living in truth.

Developing Trust between Your Adult and Child

Just as the Child needs to learn to trust that the Adult will be present in a loving way, so the Adult needs to learn to trust the Child. Often, when people first start the process of getting to know their Child, they discover that they hate their Child. They may see their Child as a helpless, powerless victim, or they may see their Child as mean, angry, and vindictive. They may believe that their Child is stupid, or empty and boring. The problem is that all they know of their Child is their abandoned Child, and they believe that this is who their Child really is. They may remember beating up other kids when they were little, or doing poorly in school, or being totally unconscious and unaware, or stealing, or starting fires, or lying; they may remember getting yelled at a lot and being told they were nothing but troublemakers. They do not realize that the Child they remember is the abandoned Child, and that they have no idea who their Child is when it is being loved. So they do not trust their Child and may feel afraid to get to know it.

The only way to overcome this mistrust is to risk getting to know this Child. A helpful way to start is to imagine that you have adopted a five-year-old child. This child has been abandoned and maybe abused, and is very angry and tough, or absent and numb, or passive and depressed. This child is not about to let you see who he or she is. What would you do? Would you tell this child he or she is a rotten kid, or would you be soft and gentle, giving this abandoned child time to feel safe? As you look into that little child's eyes, you see the fear, but you also see beyond the fear to the softness and the need for love. This is your Inner Child, perhaps angry, hard, tough, closed off, but inside he or she just wants to be loved by you. And when you love this Child long enough, he or she will open and let you in on the curiosity, creativity, passion, aliveness, playfulness, wisdom, tenderness, and sense of wonder that is who you really are.

CHAPTER 9

Getting Stuck—Getting Unstuck

We need to accept that in the end it is not our parents or God who have abandoned us; we have abandoned ourselves.

. . . many of our defenses are really our oldest friends—tried and true. They have stood by us, protected us when all else failed. And even though now they do us little good, we are reluctant to discard them.

12 Steps to Self-Parenting
PHILIP OLIVER-DIAZ AND PATRICIA A. O'GORMAN

We have seen in our work with clients that some people, upon understanding how profound and life-changing it can be for them to learn to love and connect with their Inner Child, get right down to work. They read books, they practice dialoguing every day, they pay attention to the messages from their Child, they begin to act in their Child's behalf, and they progress very rapidly. They make a commitment to themselves to learn how to be a loving Adult with their Inner Child, and they follow through. It is truly a privilege and a joy to work with these people.

Other people, however, seem to have great difficulty making the commitment and following through. They come in week after week, stuck in the same place, feeling the same misery. Or they pretend to get better to get the approval of the therapist, but it soon becomes apparent that nothing is really happening—no real work is being done. They may even be doing their dialoguing, but only as an exercise, with no real compassion and no true intent to learn.

Why are some people open to learning and taking responsibility for themselves while others are not?

By nature, human beings are committed. When you find yourself stuck, it is because in some area of your life you have been committed to avoiding or denying the fears and pain that lie there. They can be tricky to see. After years of your commitment to covering them up, your pain, fears, and beliefs are deeply buried and have probably become triggering mechanisms to go blind and unconscious. It's as if we pour all of our energy into creating a shield of invisibility, designed to hide our pain, fears, and shame-based beliefs from everybody including ourselves—and only when we recommit our energies to seeing, accepting, and experiencing the buried pain and grief will all that power be available again to help us clean up the mess and move on into creating joy and fun. The power to get unstuck is there, misdirected at present. To get unstuck you must change your commitment from avoiding responsibility for your pain and joy to being responsible for all your feelings through the intent to learn about your pain, fears, and beliefs and about what brings you joy. This recommitment must come from your Adult, since the Adult is the choicemaker regarding intent.

Your abandoned Child will probably be afraid to help you do this. No child wants to go to the hospital for an operation. But if an appendix operation is necessary to live and be healthy and grow, that choice must be made by the adult in charge. And like any loving adult, you may need to have a few long conversations with an extremely angry and frightened child. It's your job to hold on to your new commitment of uncovering the truth and at the same time be there for the Child who may be overwhelmed by fears and misinformation.

There are many fears and false beliefs that can block the willingness to learn and to taking personal responsibility. We are listing here the major fears and beliefs that we've discovered block learning in the hopes that if you find yourself stuck, these awarenesses will help you get unstuck.

Fear of the Child's Anger

When we were little children many of us suffered at the hands of our parents, grandparents, siblings, other relatives, teachers, or peers. We may have been physically, sexually, and/or emotionally abused. Not only were we powerless to protect ourselves but generally we weren't allowed to express our anger, or were further abused if we did. Most of us have old unexpressed anger and rage held within the feelings of the abandoned Child, anger at others for abandoning us as children, and at ourselves for abandoning our Inner Child and leaving the Child to take care of itself.

When you open to learning with your Child, you must be prepared to experience and express this anger and rage.

Many people are afraid of their anger. They judge their anger, telling their Inner Child that it is bad and wrong for them to feel this way, and they are afraid others will judge them too. They may be afraid their anger will get them into trouble as it did when they were children. They may believe that anger just breeds more anger. They may be afraid that they are basically angry people and have a bottomless pit of anger that will never go away no matter how much work they do. They may be afraid their anger will overwhelm them and that if they open to it they will hurt themselves or others or actually kill someone. This fear comes from their experience of being an abandoned Child with no Adult to set limits. Our experience is that anger gets out of hand only when people repress it and avoid dealing with it. Once they get in touch with their loving Adult, they can learn to discharge their anger in harmless ways. But if you believe that people will judge you, or that your anger will get you into trouble, or that it will overwhelm you, and if you are unwilling to test the validity of these beliefs, then you will stay stuck.

Most people, when they start to dialogue, come up against their Inner Child's anger at the Inner Adult for having abandoned it. This anger may go on for weeks, and if you are not willing to allow your Child to express it, you will get stuck. Julie, a small blonde woman in one of our groups, had been stuck like this. When she finally accepted the anger, she had a wonderful experience with her Child:

Julie: I just want to share some stuff. I'm feeling really excited because I've been dialoguing every day.

Group: Yay! Great, Julie! (some applause)

Julie: And I *love* it, I really *love* it. I had to get through this horrible resistance and the blocks and all this garbage. But I finally did it, and I've been doing it every day, and now I feel like I can't miss a day.

Margie: I was going to ask you what had changed. Your energy is much different today.

Group: Yes, more bubbly, lighter.

Julie: I had this incredible experience with it yesterday. Something shifted after group last week. I had started doing it, and all I was getting was that the Child was angry at the Adult. And you said, "Of course. If you had abandoned a child for this many years of her life, she'd be angry at you, too." So that put another perspective on it, and I realized, okay, then I just have to stay with that and just go through it, whatever it is. So I did. I went through that, and there was some more anger, and then something shifted! Something just shifted. And suddenly, it was like my Adult could be there in this really loving way. So yesterday, I was asking my Child what she wanted. And she wanted to go into the rolling hills where there was lots of grass and take my dogs and just go out and spend the day. First, I don't know any place like that right now and second, I don't have the time. So I thought, well, I've always heard that if you do things as a visualization using all the senses, the mind has the same experience as if you were actually doing it. And I decided, okay, I'm just going to do this visualization. So I went into my room and put on beautiful music and I did an incredible visualization of this experience. It was just incredible. I got totally into it, and then I got into all this sadness and grief, because it really connected me to what my little girl didn't get, the sadness of what she didn't get. But even that was incredible, to have that flow so freely. And that was yesterday.

It is important to understand that there are two kinds of anger, closed anger and open anger, that is, anger expressed with the intent to protect and anger expressed with the intent to learn. Closed anger is the controlling or vindictive anger that is expressed by the abandoned Child when no loving Inner Adult shows up and the Inner Child feels helpless and powerless. Closed anger is also the anger expressed by the unloving Adult towards the abandoned Child. This is the anger that is frightening and can get out of control, harming oneself and others. Open anger is the anger expressed by the abandoned Child when the loving Inner Adult intends to learn about and understand what the Inner Child has experienced in the past or is experiencing in the present. The Inner Adult is there to place limits on the behavior, making sure you don't harm yourself and others. The loving Adult listens and provides comfort and support for the Child's feelings of rage. This is the anger that opens and teaches and helps to heal old wounds.

Fear of the Child's Pain

Underneath anger is always pain. All of us experienced pain as children, and we all learned how to keep from feeling it. But the feelings are still there within the Inner Child. In order to learn with the

Inner Child, you must be willing to feel and heal the old pain. If you still hold your abandoned Child's or unloving Adult's false beliefs about pain (if you open to it, it will be unending, it will overwhelm you, you will die or go crazy, you just can't handle it), and if you are unwilling to test these beliefs, then you will get stuck in a protective mode. You cannot open to learning and protect yourself from your pain at the same time.

Often we are unwilling to even know about our old pain. If you are invested in believing that you had an ideal childhood, if your family trained you to keep secrets, then you may believe that it is wrong to become aware of the truth. Until knowing the truth is more important than hiding and living in denial, you will stay stuck. Most of us will experience deep grief when we come to terms with the loss of our idealized parents and our idealized childhood. Unless we are willing to go through this pain and grief, no recovery is possible. There is no way around pain, fear, and grief. We have to go through these feelings to heal.

The deepest pain that we have to face is the aloneness and loneliness and the wrenching experience of powerlessness with respect to those feelings that we experienced as children. All our craziness is caused by our reluctance to experience these feelings. All our ego protections start with the fear of that pain. Below is a poem that Erika wrote as she was confronting her own childhood loneliness.

> Loneliness is the only pure pain.
>   All other pain is born of it.
>   It alone
>   ultimately fathers every
>   conceivable protection against it.
>
>   We begin to wither at its mere mention.
>   It is the ultimate Separation
>   of the soul
>   from humanity.
>
>   It is what we fear we cannot survive,
>   For it is the hurt we alone
>   Cannot repair.
>   Loneliness is a fissure of the heart
>   that can be bridged only by another.
>   We inflict it,
>   despise it,
>   and deny it,

> Never realizing
> That in its presence
> We are forced to move forward . . .
> Loneliness
>   is the book
>   we refuse to read . . .

Our deepest loneliness, which is "bridged only by another," cannot begin to be healed until we first create the bridge within ourselves, the connection between our Adult and our Child. Another's love has no place to enter until your own heart is open. Until you face your pain, you will protect yourself against it and your heart will be closed.

Facing the pain of your loneliness, aloneness, and powerlessness takes great courage and will not be accomplished until there is a solid connection between your Inner Adult and your Inner Child. Your Child will not let you feel this pain until it trusts that you will not run away from the pain, that you will stay and provide loving support to learn from and move through this pain.

Erika uses a metaphor to describe her experience of opening to this pain.

It was like taking my boat out to a very deep part of the ocean, 14,000 feet, and jumping into the water. Most people spend their lives frantically trying to stay on the surface, fearing that if they let go they will drown. Or they lie quietly on the surface on their backs, as if they are dead, in a state of depression, so as not to face their fears of pain. But facing aloneness is like letting go and letting yourself sink to the bottom, down 14,000 feet. You go down slowly. At first you hold your breath, but then you find you can breathe under water. You don't know where the bottom is, so you just have to go on faith that everything will be all right. Finally you hit bottom and look around and see what it is you've been afraid of feeling and knowing your whole life. You might stay there for awhile, maybe a month or so until you've learned all there is to learn, and then you start to feel lighter. Slowly you rise back to the surface. There may be other times in your life when you need to let go and sink in again, but it will not last as long and you will never again be afraid of it. You will probably never again have to go all the way to the bottom.

The unwillingness to feel and experience the pain that lies within the Inner Child is one of the main reasons people get stuck. As long as it is more important to protect yourself against feeling and being responsible for learning about the beliefs and experiences that created and continue to create your pain than it is to learn, you will not be able to learn.

Sometimes, even when the Adult has decided to be open to learning about the Child's anger and pain, the person still feels stuck. This may be because the Inner Child is afraid that the Adult will judge its anger and pain. When this is the case, the Inner Child will remain silent until it feels it can truly rely on the Inner Adult to be loving.

Fear of Being Controlled and Betrayed by the Child

People who learned to resist as children to protect themselves from being controlled by a parent, grandparent, or sibling often bring this way of being into adulthood. They become so conditioned to resisting anything that someone wants of them that they unconsciously resist the wants and needs of their own Inner Child. Your Inner Child wants and needs your attention, love, and approval, as well as your intent to learn with and from it and your devotion to its comfort, sense of security, and joy. It *always* wants and needs these things from you. If you are a resistant person, you might find yourself unconsciously saying to your Inner Child, "I don't have to do what you say. Just because you want it, doesn't mean I have to give it to you. Get someone else to give it to you."

Below is part of a session Margie had with Dean, who discovered that he had been stuck in a power struggle with his Inner Child.

Dean's Adult: What do you want right now?

Dean's Child: I want you to pay attention to me. I want you to talk to me. I want you to listen to me and not ignore me . . . if that isn't too much to ask (annoyed sigh). I'm angry at you because you say that you're doing all these things but you're not. I'm fed up with how you treat me, and I feel so alone and cut off from you. When are you going to make the decision, for god's sake, when are you going to change it? (really angry).

Margie: Go back there [to being the Adult].

Dean's Adult: (sigh) It's so easy to say I don't know when I'm going to change it and just put it off and put it off and put it off. Because I haven't made that decision. It's hard to open up to what you keep inside and have kept inside, because I haven't let you get it out. And I feel really unsure about making that commitment to you. I know that I've never been able to do that. I've always blamed somebody else for that; I've never taken that responsibility. And I can see how everything's just getting worse because of it. I still feel unsure about doing it.

Margie: Come back here.

Dean's Child: You're doing it *again*! You're being the same stupid asshole that you've always been. You're just making excuses again. I don't even want to talk to you when you do that because there's no point. You don't listen to me and then I end up feeling bad, and it gets worse and worse and worse. And I'm just trapped inside here. It's like you're never, ever, ever going to do anything about it. You're just going to leave me in here, and I'm never going to get to do or be anything except what's already been. If you're not going to do anything about it, then what's the point?

Margie: Now move back into your Adult. . . . Your Child is telling you that you're a child abuser, and he feels there's no point in living this way. But of course you have to continue to resist so that you won't be controlled by him.

Dean's Adult: Is that what I'm doing?

Margie: It feels like a power struggle to me. It feels like an intense internal power struggle. He wants this from you so badly, and you will not give it to him. You will not be controlled by your Child. Feels like you'll give lip service, you'll talk it, you'll act like you're aware and all that stuff, but meanwhile the most important thing is to resist, to not commit, to not do it, to just resist what he wants of you.

Dean: Feels like I can't even say the words that I can commit to it.

Margie: I know. That's what makes me feel like it's a power struggle.

Dean: It feels like being a yoyo. It feels like backwards and forwards with the same thing.

Margie: Yes. Can you feel your resistance?

Dean: Uh huh.

Margie: Well, that resistance is the power struggle within yourself. Your little boy wants so much for you to pay attention to him, and you're not about to, because you're not going to give in to him.

Dean: It does have that feeling of giving in, if he wants me to do it and I do it.

Margie: Yeah, that's what it feels like, if you do it, you're giving in.

Dean: Yeah.

Margie: In your effort not to be controlled by your Child, you are being totally controlled because you're not making an independent decision about what you want. Can you honestly say to me "I don't want to be a loving human being"?

Dean: No.

Margie: Well then, if that's not the truth and you do want to be a loving human being . . .

Dean: . . . then why am I not doing it?

Margie: . . . then you're not making that independent choice. Feels like giving in rather than an independent choice.

Dean: Giving in to myself . . .

Margie: Yes.

Dean: Giving in to my Child.

Margie: Right. That's right.

Dean: I suppose that's the ultimate power struggle, isn't it?

After this session Dean became committed to dialoguing with his Child and began to make real progress.

Often the power struggles that began in childhood get projected onto a mate, one's own child, or even one's therapist. Bob and Rachael came in for marriage counseling, because they were feeling very disconnected from each other. They were fighting a lot and sex between them was nonexistent, something that Bob was very unhappy about.

Bob believed that there was something wrong with Rachael because she was angry most of the time and uninterested in sex. Rachael, on the other hand, was angry at Bob and believed the problems were all his fault.

At the beginning of therapy it appeared as if Bob was a very open person. He seemed soft and gentle and very able to make himself happy. He had lots of hobbies that he rarely pursued because Rachael would feel rejected when he didn't spend all of his spare time with her. Rachael was always angry at Bob, always blaming him for her unhappiness. During one of the sessions, she became so angry and blaming and in such denial about her intent to protect that the therapist suggested that the sessions would not help her until she decided to learn. She yelled that she did want to learn and then terminated therapy. Bob continued for a few more sessions. He was just beginning to become aware of his Inner Child and of how angry his Child was at his mother for always trying to control him when he suddenly quit therapy. The following week, Rachael showed up at his time. She sat down with a resolute look and said, "You were right. I have been angry and closed, and it's making me very unhappy. I'm tired of being unhappy. I'm ready to work." Needless to say, the therapist was quite surprised.

In the next six weeks Rachael made incredible progress. She was diligent about doing her dialogues, and connecting with her Inner Child became her highest priority. As she began to see clearly how to make her Inner Child happy and how not to take other people's behavior personally, her anger melted and she began to feel happy and peaceful inside. But the happier she became, the angrier Bob became. Their relationship was getting worse. The therapist asked Rachael to come in with Bob, if he was willing.

Bob showed up with Rachael, but he was very tense, cold, and distant. Like Rachael had previously been, he denied his intent to protect against feeling his fear. Rachael said that whenever she tried to share her Inner Child work with Bob and let him know how much it was doing for her, he would become irritated. The therapist asked Bob how he felt about Rachael's change; he said he didn't trust it. Suddenly he started blaming her in the same angry way that she used to blame him. In the midst of this he blurted out, "The two of you are ganging up on me! You feel just like my mother. You just want to control me and get me to do things your way. Well, your way isn't the only way. My way is different from your way, and I don't have to do it your way." The therapist pointed out that he was in a power struggle with both her and Rachael and asked, "Does it feel like if you open to learning about your Inner Child that you are capitulating, giving in, losing, being controlled?" "Yes," he said, wide-eyed. "That's exactly what it feels like. So that's what's happening."

Just because Bob realized he was in a power struggle did not mean he got unstuck. He stayed stuck until he was willing to test out his fear that he would lose himself and be controlled by Rachael and the therapist if he opened to learning with and from his Inner Child.

We've noticed that clients who resist doing their inner work, who resist learning with and taking responsibility for their Child often say things like:

"This process is really dumb."

"This theory is too simplistic."

"Who says your way is the right way?"

"I don't buy this Adult-Child junk. What do you think I am, schizophrenic?"

"I've done all sorts of different therapies and workshops. None of them have worked. Why should this be any different? So why bother? It won't work."

"I don't know how."

Many of us have false beliefs about who the Inner Child really is, because all we know is the child when it is unloved and abandoned. You may believe that your Child is a troublemaker, wild and unruly, unwilling to ever follow any rules. You may feel sure that he or she just wants control over you and that if you open to your Child you will be out of control of your life.

Thomas, a client of ours, has an authoritarian Inner Adult who treats his Inner Child just like his parents did. Thomas has always followed the rules, one of which is that he never miss work, even when he is sick. Thomas has been afraid to dialogue with his Inner Child for fear his Child wants him to break the rules and cause chaos in his life. His Child does want to break some rules, but breaking these rules would certainly not cause chaos. Thomas had the following dialogue in our office with his Child. It was a cold and rainy day, and Thomas, who had just come from work, had a cold.

Adult: Why do you hate the rain?

Child: I just do. I hate it. I hate it. I hate the cold. It makes me feel alone.

Adult: So the main reason you hate the rain is the cold and feeling alone? How can I help you?

Child: Keep me warm. And keep me home from work sometimes when it rains, especially when I'm sick.

Thomas did not want to know that his Child felt like this. Not wanting to know kept him from dialoguing. He was afraid if he listened to his Child, his Child would take over and Thomas would end up being an irresponsible person. Until Thomas wants to know the truth and moves into an intent to learn, he is stuck.

Many people fear that if they open to their Inner Child they won't want to work anymore, that they will get lazy and shirk their responsibilities. They believe all the Child wants to do is play or hide or fight or cry all the time. This may be true when they've abandoned their Child, but is certainly not true when their Child is feeling loved by them. Yet they fear that if they open to knowing their unloved Child, they will end up being controlled by this Child and lose everything. This is a false belief. We've never seen this occur as a result of people opening to their Inner Child. In fact, we've seen the opposite happen. As people connect with the aliveness of their Inner Child and help to heal its fear and pain, they become more productive and creative. They may go through an initial period of confusion, resistance, and loss of efficiency, but this is temporary. You will not know this about yourself, however, until you are willing to test your fears by deciding to learn with your Inner Child.

This lack of trust in the Child was well illustrated in a session with Shelly, a nineteen-year-old college student. Near the end of the previous session, it had become apparent that Shelly was having some difficulty about her feelings toward her father. The therapist had asked Shelly to dialogue with her Child about this at home, but Shelly got stuck behind her fear of loss of control, of being controlled by her Child and did not dialogue. Shelly was afraid that her Child didn't ever want to spend time with her father, and Adult Shelly believed that if her Child felt that way, then she had to go along with her Child. As she dialogued in the session it became apparent that this is not how her Child felt—that little Shelly just didn't like it when big Shelly abandoned her around her father. But even if her Child didn't want to be around her father and Adult Shelly did, it would not mean that Adult Shelly would have to be controlled by her Child. It would mean that Shelly would need to open to learning about why her Child felt this way and how she could help her feel better in that situation. Shelly realized from this session that she makes a lot of assumptions about her Child's feelings and then doesn't want to know what they really are (and that she does this with other people as well). She realized that she sees her Child as a demanding, overbearing, troublesome Child, the way her parents saw her, rather than as a Child who needs to be listened to and understood.

Our ego always wants to be in control and fears losing control. It tells us that if we open to the Child we will be out of control. This is terrifying to most people, so the unloving Adult wants control over the Child. In turn, the unloved Child wants control over others and over feelings. As infants we felt so out of control. We couldn't walk or talk or do anything to get our own needs met, and if no one heard us cry and left us alone, we could have died. Now, as adults, the ego tells us that we could die if we are out of control, especially out of control over being abandoned, out of control over being in pain. *The fear of losing control over the people and events that cause pain and the fear of losing control over the experience of pain is one of the major blocks to learning.* Until we are willing to feel our pain, we will opt for control over ourselves, others, and the outcome of events. Many people are *addicted* to control, erroneously believing that having control and resisting being controlled is what will make them happy. To learn, we have to *surrender* that control to our Higher Selves, and this is where so many people get stuck. We cannot move into our Higher Selves without opening to knowing the Inner Child, and for many people this makes them feel so out of control over their lives and their feelings that they are unwilling to do it. Until you are willing to risk knowing what happens when you surrender control to your Higher Self, you will stay stuck.

Below is part of a session with Ed.

Ed: When I talk to my Child, it feels as if my Adult is really controlling and criticizing and doing things like that. I'm not sure exactly how to do an exploration going back and forth between my Adult and my Child, because it feels as if he . . . I don't know how to put this into words. I guess I'm uncomfortable with my Child advising my Adult. It's like taking advice from my kids! I really don't trust it! It feels like I do all the exploring with my Adult, my Adult talking to my Adult, instead of to my Child.

Therapist: Sounds like you want to control him instead of learn with him.

Ed: Yeah. Like shut him up completely. I see that.

Therapist: So you feel out of control if you let yourself be guided by your Higher Self?

Ed: Oh. You're *being led*, you're not leading?

Therapist: Right. You're surrendering to the information that comes through your loved Child from your Higher Self. Your ego is not in control of it.

Ed: That makes me real nervous. In fact, that is one of the problems when I talk to my Child, I feel like . . . *I don't want to know that!!!*

Therapist: So this is a conflict between your ego and your Higher Self. Your ego wants control.

Ed: And I've got a really strong ego.

Therapist: Yes. Your ego does not want to give up control and be guided. To open to your Child you have to be willing to let go of the ego belief that it knows what is right for you or for anybody else. You have to be willing to surrender to the universal love and guidance which comes through the Child. I see an enormous conflict in you that you haven't come to terms with. Your ego says, "I'm gonna do it *myself*. Don't tell me what to do. I know what is right. I know what is best and I'm going to do it *myself*, Goddammit . . . *if it kills me!!!*"

Ed: It's like a stubborn little kid.

Therapist: But you have the power to make another choice. Your Adult is the choicemaker. Your Adult has chosen your ego over your Higher Self.

Ed: Uh huh. Over and over and over again.

Therapist: Why? What are you afraid of if you surrender and allow yourself to be guided? What might happen? What are you afraid of losing?

Ed: I guess . . . well, approval, for one thing, from my family and friends.

Therapist: What else?

Ed: I guess I'm feeling the pressure to fit the mold of a happily married, two-kid family and live in a house and make money.

Therapist: You're really afraid of what he wants. You keep shutting him out because you don't know what he wants, and you think what he wants is weird and threatening and wild and crazy and you're terrified.

Ed: I'm not even sure if I'm afraid of what he wants, because I don't know what he wants.

Therapist: But you can't know until you take the judgment off and until you're willing to lose approval. He isn't going to tell you if he feels you're afraid of what he is going to say. Until you are ready to say, "I will be guided, no matter what the loss. To gain my self, I will lose whatever I need to lose. But I want to gain my self in a pure and loving way. And I'm willing to lose whatever I have to lose to get it." Until you're ready to make that choice, then you've opted for control.

Ed: Well, I know the stuff he has told me, which has not been a whole lot, but whatever he has told me has worked out perfectly and has felt really good.

Therapist: Yes. You see, the guidance is unerring.

Ed: Yeah.

Therapist: And what will really bring you joy in life might surprise you. And you're not going to know what it is until you're willing to be guided and let go of control. That is what the twelve-step programs are all about. Surrendering control. You can't manage it all by yourself. You have to surrender to a Higher Source.

Ed: It feels really scary. Really, really scary.

Therapist: What are you frightened of? So far the worst you've come up with is your family's disapproval. What else are you afraid of?

Ed: Well, I guess I'm afraid of losing everything. That is what it comes down to. I'm afraid that I don't love Rebecca, that I don't want to be with my kids, that I'll go off to Africa . . . you know, do something wild like live with the natives and show them how to build houses or something like that. I doubt that something like that would happen, but I guess that is the real fear. That it will be *that* life-changing . . .

Until Ed is willing to surrender and begin to learn with his Inner Child, he will never find out what really brings him joy.

Fear of Being Responsible for One's Self

Many people will go to almost any length to get love and approval from others, or avoid their disapproval, believing (mistakenly) that approval will make them happy and that they can somehow *control* getting the approval and avoiding the disapproval. Perhaps you believe it is more important to *get* love than to *give* it, to be *seen* rather than to *see*, that it's the love and approval of others that *really matters*. Many people mistakenly believe that their *best feeling* comes from getting something from someone else—connection, attention, sex, approval, understanding, acceptance, love—rather than realizing that their best feeling comes from giving love and understanding to themselves and others. They believe that their best feeling comes from outside themselves, rather than from inside. When you believe this, you find yourself always wanting more and more from someone or something—more sex, affection, attention, approval, or time with someone; or more food, drugs, alcohol, material possessions, money, or power—and never feeling that what you're getting is enough. This false belief is at the heart of addiction and codependence.

There are times when a person is stuck because he or she is deeply addicted to another person. Such people believe at a very deep level that their best feelings come from this other person; they can't imagine generating such feelings by themselves. They may believe that it's not their job to take care of themselves emotionally, that this other person is *supposed* to do it. One of our clients discovered this belief when he heard himself say to his Inner Child, "I don't want this job. It's not my job. It's Tessa's job. She's supposed to do it. That's why I'm with her." When this is the case, you may need to leave the relationship and be alone to get unstuck. Just as an alcoholic needs to abstain from alcohol to begin healing, so a relationship addict needs to abstain from relationships. Seeking another relationship will result in the same addiction, until you decide it is your own responsibility to learn to connect deeply and lovingly with your own Inner Child and experience feelings that are *better* than those achieved *from* another person. Only then can you experience the truly wonderful feelings that come from sharing your love *with* another person, rather than just getting love *from* another person.

Some people get stuck because they are constantly seeking in others the love they never received from their parents. Stacy, a client of ours, said in a session, "I yearn to get from someone what I didn't get from my parents. I'm always looking for someone to make up to me what I lost out on. It doesn't seem fair that I should have to give that to myself. I don't want to do it. If I do it for myself, then I'll forever lose out on someone doing it for me." Stacy refuses to accept that another's love cannot even be experienced by her until she opens and loves herself. Her unloving behavior toward herself, which closes down her heart, blocks out love from others.

Perhaps you act loving only *after* getting another's love and approval *first*, convincing yourself that you deserve it and that others do not deserve your love until they prove they love you. Perhaps you believe you're already loving, so that that's not where the problem is—it's not with you, it's with others. You may see yourself as so loving that if only your partner would let you love him or her, everything would be fine. Many people who are disconnected never see themselves as unloving to themselves or to others. They are stuck because they don't admit how unloving they are. They may know how to *act* loving in the world, so that others may think they are loving, but the primary people in their lives don't feel loved by them. They are stuck because they are lying to themselves about their intent, which is to *get love before giving it*. They *act* loving to get love. The primary intent is still to get love from others rather than give it to themselves and others, and the more miserable they become, the greater their demand for love.

Underneath, they are afraid of taking responsibility for themselves, because of their belief, which they absorbed from their parents, that they are *incapable* of taking care of themselves and making themselves happy. Sometimes these people are completely unaware of the fact that they have an Adult who is abdicating responsibility. They often say, "I don't have a small Child *in* me—I *am* the Child." The Adult has so completely abdicated responsibility that the Child is abandoned, believing that no Adult exists. These people often say, in response to why they are not doing the dialoguing, "I can't. I don't know how." This is the abandoned Child speaking, who truly cannot initiate the dialogue, who truly does not know how. Until the Adult recognizes its own existence and its choice to be an unloving Adult and to avoid responsibility for the feelings and needs of the Inner Child, and its power to make a different choice, then that individual is stuck. Erika tells how she has seen people appear to be stuck in this way in her therapy practice.

I have a springer spaniel named Chi who is sometimes a great teacher for stuck people. Chi is often in sessions with me. She is wonderful at helping people's Inner Child feel comfortable by offering unconditional love in the form of hugs and kisses.

I have noticed that how people respond to Chi's affection is often inconsistent with how they treat their Inner Child. What is puzzling is that the very people who cherish Chi and play with her or kiss her will get themselves so stuck that they turn to me and say, "But I just don't know how to love my Inner Child!" At that moment Chi usually helps us confront that erroneous belief. Loving their Inner Child is no different than the way they feel about and treat Chi. They already know how—it's just a matter of choice. Convincing yourself that you don't know how to feel and behave in a loving way is one of the ego's biggest lies.

Often people with these false beliefs allow their fun-loving Child to come out only when they feel safe and approved of, or when they are trying to get approval by being entertaining. Anytime they feel the slightest bit threatened, the angry, hurt, abandoned Child is left with no Inner Adult to help it not take things personally or to prevent it from acting out in angry, vindictive, violent, or self-destructive ways. The unloving Adult then perpetuates the disconnection by blaming the abandoned Child for feeling threatened and acting out.

Dorothy is a very attractive woman in her late forties. She has been married for a long time and has two grown sons. She stayed home with her children until they both left home and then got a job as a secretary. She came into therapy because she found out that her husband, Paul, was having an affair. Paul is a lawyer and is having an affair with a fellow lawyer, Pamela, an intelligent and interesting woman. Paul has told Dorothy outright that he has no intention of ending the affair. He has told her that he still loves her, but he is tired of her attempts to control him and make him responsible for her feelings. He has told her he is bored with her inability to carry on an interesting and intelligent conversation and bored with her lack of interest in learning about her own inner processes.

Dorothy is a very bright woman, and there is no reason why she can't learn, other than the fact that she believes she can't. She believes she is very limited. She understands what "intent to learn" means, and she has been taught how to do the dialogues between her Adult and

Child, but she does not do them. Instead, she pretends that she is happy. At least once a week she blows up at Paul and threatens to leave him, but she never does. She is constantly trying to manipulate him into giving her more attention. Paul is feeling more and more bullied by Dorothy; his loving feelings for her are dwindling. Meanwhile, his relationship with Pamela is growing stronger. He says he enjoys being with Dorothy when she is being playful, but he is getting very tired of her abandoned Child, who tries to get him to take responsibility for her. He no longer wants that responsibility. He wants an equal relationship with someone who can relate to him from Adult and Child. He is beginning to think about leaving Dorothy.

Even in the face of losing Paul, whom she says she loves, Dorothy refuses to face her fear of responsibility for herself. She maintains that she is "incapable" of being an Adult for her abandoned Child and refuses to practice the inner connection. She has even fooled herself into believing that she is doing the dialoguing, but she only writes from her Child. She is afraid to test out her belief that she is incapable of being a responsible Adult for her Inner Child, and she refuses to face this fear, choosing to try to control Paul instead. Dorothy is stuck. She will not get unstuck until she recommits to becoming fully responsible for herself and acting in her own behalf in spite of her fears and beliefs, which is unlikely to happen until she hits bottom. People in Dorothy's position seldom shift until their lives are falling apart, until their protections are no longer working for them at all.

Fear of Discovering Your Core Self is Unlovable

Many people were not only *told* that they were bad when they were children—but some of them *did* bad things. Perhaps you really acted out as a child, beating up other kids, stealing, lying, starting fires, or generally being mean. This may be who you are when you feel unloved and abandoned, but it is not who you really are, who your Inner Child is when feeling loved. But if you believe that who you really are is bad, then you might be afraid to learn about your Inner Child and find out the truth. *The core of us is never bad*, but you will not know this until you risk opening to learning, feeling the pain, and remembering. As long as you fear finding out, you will stay stuck.

Many of us grow up believing that who we are is *not worth knowing*. If your parents were completely uninterested in knowing you, knowing your fears and desires, your joys and pain, then you might believe that your Inner Child is just not worth knowing, so why bother to learn with it? When you believe this, you might find yourself persuading others to want to know you, believing that only if they want to know you are you worth knowing. Until you are willing to get to know your Inner Child and find out that your belief that you are not worth knowing is indeed a false one, you will stay stuck.

Shame is the feeling we have when we believe that our core is bad, or that something about us is bad. Our feelings of shame will not be healed until we open to loving our Inner Child and discover how truly lovable we really are, underneath all those protections. When we fear that we are bad, then we naturally fear that others will see us as bad or wrong. The fear of being judged as *wrong* is often a block to learning with others. When we believe that our Inner Child is bad, then we believe we need to control our Child around others so as not to be rejected, and we are generally closed to others' feedback, falsely believing that we can thus protect ourselves from being seen as wrong.

Fear of Knowing the Truth

You may fear that if you are open to knowing your Child, you will find that it wants things that your Adult doesn't necessarily want or things that conflict with what your Adult wants. Perhaps your Child wants to settle down and have a family, but your Adult wants to devote all your time to building your career. Perhaps your Adult wants to spend time with people whom your Child doesn't like to be around. Perhaps your Child hates your work, or feels a lack of integrity in your work, or hates your long hours, but your Adult wants to keep doing it for economic reasons. Perhaps your Child wants to go into therapy and your Adult thinks therapy is a waste of time. As with any conflict between two people, these can be worked out when the Adult chooses to learn, but you may be afraid that if you are open to your Child, one of you will win and the other will lose. Dr. John K. Pollard, in *Self-Parenting*, gives a wonderful example of an internal conflict and how it was worked out. In this case, the Adult wanted to go to a weekend seminar for his work, but the Child did not want to work twelve days in a row. Instead, the Child wanted to go skiing on the weekend. Pollard makes the point that if the Adult ignores the Child, the Child is likely to sabotage the situation by making the Adult sick, so that he would have to go to the seminar sick or cancel it, in which case the Child could have a miraculous recovery and get to do what he wants. But when the Adult decided to work it out with the Child, he discovered that he didn't mind taking Thursday and Friday off work and going skiing so that he could attend the seminar over the weekend. There is always a way to resolve inner conflict, but if you fear it will always be a win-lose situation, and you are not willing to test out this fear, then you will stay stuck.

Regina, an accountant, came into therapy because she was very depressed. She had stopped seeing her friends and found herself just sitting home alone every night. She couldn't figure out why. As we talked it became apparent that, while she loved being an accountant, her Child hated where she worked because it felt like she had to do things that lacked integrity. But Regina had just bought a new house and her Adult was worried that if she changed jobs she wouldn't make enough money to support the house. After realizing that her Child was causing the depression, she decided to rent out part of the house and change jobs. Once her Child realized that she was being heard, the depression lifted.

Clinton, a businessman, also came in because he was depressed. It turned out his Child was unhappy because all he did was work and his Child never got to play. When this man realized that his depression came from his Child's desire for playtime and companionship, he quit therapy. He didn't want to face his inner conflict. He had always believed that making lots of money would make him happy, and he wasn't ready to face the truth.

Often the intent to learn gets blocked behind a fear of knowing how you really feel about something and knowing that if you let yourself know the truth, you will have to do something about it. It may seem easier and safer to stay unconscious about what you really want, especially if what you want means taking a risk.

Carol came into therapy because she was very depressed. She complained that she felt tired and drained and was always getting sick. She had been having back trouble and had been seeing a physical therapist. She had been married for twenty years and believed she had a good marriage, although she was sexually uninterested in her husband and didn't really enjoy spending time with him. She had tried for years to establish an emotional connection with him, but he was cold and distant much of the time, especially when she refused to have sex.

The therapist taught Carol how to do the dialoguing and suggested that Carol ask her Child how she felt about her husband. The Child answered, "I don't want this marriage to end." The Adult responded with, "Neither do I." Carol spent the next few months learning about her codependence. She made quite a bit of progress in breaking away from caretaking, but she wasn't feeling any better. The therapist encouraged her to dialogue with her Child, but each week she had another reason why she didn't do it. It became apparent that she was stuck. She didn't want to know her Child.

Finally, a few months after starting therapy, the therapist suggested that Carol again ask her Child how she felt about her husband. This time the Child said, "I hate him! He's so mean. He doesn't love me. He's never loved me. He just wants me to love him. He never cares about how I feel. He just wants to use me for sex, and I hate it when you let him use me." Carol was stunned. This was the truth she was trying so hard to avoid knowing. Because she didn't want to face her fears of leaving her marriage, she didn't want to know how she really felt. She got unstuck only when she was willing to know the truth and face her fears.

Sometimes the way people avoid facing an inner conflict is to assume they already know what their Child is feeling and wanting. Their unloving Adult takes an arrogant and controlling position and says, "I already know what my Child is feeling, so why bother asking?" This way the Adult can make the decisions without ever having to consult the Child, and the inner conflict is avoided. But it cannot be avoided forever. Eventually the Child will act out by causing depression or illness.

Fear of Failure

Many people have grown up without any real sense of having an Inner Child, and they do not believe there is a Child in them who has things to say to them. When asked why they are not dialoguing, they say they are afraid that they will fail at the task because "the Child won't show up," or "the Child won't have anything to say," or "there is no Child. I'm just empty inside." As long as it is more important to them to protect themselves against the possibility of failure than it is to test out the validity of their fears and beliefs, they will stay stuck behind their fear. Also, as we said earlier, many people believe they have no Adult and that they are therefore incapable of taking care of their Child. They are afraid that if they attempt to dialogue no Adult will show up, so they avoid failure by doing nothing.

Fear of Outgrowing a Relationship

If you intend to learn with your Inner Child, you will grow. You will become more powerful, secure, joyful, and loving. If you are in a relationship and your partner chooses not to do his or her inner work, there is a very good possibility that you will outgrow the relationship and eventually feel very dissatisfied with it. The more connected you become with yourself, the less you will want to be in a relationship with someone who is disconnected from him/herself and therefore from you.

Many people hold themselves back from growing for this very reason. If it is more important to you to protect your relationship than it is to become whole within yourself, then you will stay stuck behind the fear of outgrowing the relationship. You must be willing to lose everything before you will gain everything, and this is a hard place to reach. Many people find themselves holding themselves back when their children are young because they don't want to risk breaking up the family, and this is certainly understandable. It is important for them to realize, however, that they are not providing adequate role-modeling for their children, which is one of the most important things they can offer their children.

There is always the possibility that if you decide to grow, your mate will feel enough pain over being left behind that he or she will open up, but there is no guarantee of this. If you find yourself stuck, you may need to ask yourself, "Am I willing to sacrifice myself to preserve the relationship, or is it time to reach for my wholeness and risk losing the relationship?"

Willingness to Face Fear and Pain

It seems that the world is divided into two kinds of people, those who are willing to assume personal responsibility for their own happiness and unhappiness, who are willing to learn, to face their fear and pain, and to test the validity of their beliefs, and those who are unwilling to take personal responsibility and have chosen to let their fears and false beliefs control them. In other words, there are people who are committed to learning and being personally responsible, and people who are committed to protecting themselves against personal responsibility. Of course everyone is sometimes willing and sometimes not. It's important to realize that if you are willing less than 50 percent of the time, you will hardly progress at all, because the damage you do when you are disconnected can so easily cancel out the good that occurs when you are open to learning with your Child.

What does it mean to be willing? Let's use the analogy of the ski slope. You have barely learned to ski, and your instructor takes you to the top of a slope. To you it looks straight down, but your instructor assures you that you can get down safely. Of course there are no guarantees. There is always the chance that you will break a leg. You look down the slope and you are terrified. You *believe* you can't do it. What do you do? Do you take a risk, challenge your belief, and ski down the slope? Or do you take the chair back down?

People who have learned to ski have chosen to face their fear. If they hadn't been willing to face their fear, if they hadn't decided to ski, they would never have learned how. Taking the chair back down is like our addictions, like getting someone or something else to take away our fear. Many of you may have been willing to face your fear on the ski slope, but how often have you taken the chair back down in life? How often have you chosen the intent to protect instead of the intent to learn?

The more willing you are to face anxiety, loneliness, aloneness, fear, hurt, pain, boredom, disappointment, or any other discomfort, the faster you will progress through these feelings to your joy. The more you disconnect from these feelings, that is, the more often you take the chair down the slope rather than face your feelings and learn from them, the longer you will stay stuck.

It is very painful to be in a relationship with someone who is stuck. It's like watching child abuse, except that the child who is getting abused is the Inner Child. It's hard to see someone who is feeling empty, insecure, hurt, angry, depressed, dead, or ill and know that they are causing these feelings in themselves by being unloving to themselves. We want to help them, yet there is nothing we can do. *We cannot control or change another's choice.* As long as protecting against their fears is more important to them than facing their fears and their pain, they will stay stuck, and there is nothing anyone can do.

It's hard to see families break up because one or both people refuse to do their inner work. Every day as therapists we watch people continue to beat up their Inner Child and refuse to learn. It's heartbreaking. We do the best we can to help them find the courage to face their fear and pain, but when it becomes apparent that they are stuck and not willing to do anything about it, then we have to let them go.

Why are some people willing to challenge their fears and beliefs and face their deepest pain while others stay stuck in unloving behavior? The answer has to do with a person's highest priority. When your highest priority is to be loving, *when your deepest desire is to be a loving human being to yourself and others, and when you believe that it is possible to get there*, then you are on that path. The two elements to willingness, then, are *desire* and *belief*. But when self-protection is more important, then you will not move out of your stuck place, no matter how many books you read or how many workshops you attend. As therapists we know many people who read all the books, go to therapy, and attend all the workshops, and who have not moved out of their protective behavior. This is because *their fear is greater than their desire*, and their protections are still working to keep them from hitting bottom. If they finally hit bottom and experience all the pain, fear, aloneness, and failure that they have been trying to avoid with their protections, then they may begin to learn. Many people have to hit bottom before the desire to succeed is greater than the desire to avoid pain, fear, loneliness, or failure. The people who grow are those individuals whose desire to heal and to be loving and joyful is so great that they are willing to *commit* to the process of growth. It is not enough to want something. We will not get what we say we want until we are willing to commit ourselves to getting it and are willing to fail along the way to success. Each of us has the will to choose what is most important to us—to avoid pain and failure or to heal and grow and be loving. The choice we make governs everything.

CHAPTER 10

Processing with Help: Mothering

When the nurturing, receptive, and intuitive part of us is developed and we allow that depth of connection to go forth to another
human being in the way we do to our children, then we are doing
what we came here to do.

Models of Love
JOYCE AND BARRY VISSELL

Contrary to popular belief that we should be able to recover alone, we
cannot do it by ourselves. We need the feedback of others to see ourselves clearly, and we need other people to help us through our fear
and pain. Even though we may be doing a very good job of loving our
Inner Child, often our Child's pain is so great that we cannot manage
it ourselves. Sometimes we just need to be held as we go through our
pain. Sometimes we may need others around to let us know we are not
alone in our struggles. Sometimes we may need guidance in learning
how to be loving to our Inner Child.

It's important to understand the difference between *need* and
neediness. We all need the help of others to learn and grow. However,
we are being needy when we abandon our Inner Child and expect
others to fix us—to take away our pain, loneliness, and fear, or to make
us happy. Need, then, means getting help from others, while needy
means expecting others to do it for us.

The next three chapters explore various ways of receiving help from
others. The important thing to recognize is that *others cannot help us
unless we decide to learn to become a loving Adult and help ourselves.* We
cannot be helped if we abandon responsibility for our feelings to someone else, abdicating our own responsibility to our Child. Others can
love us, comfort us, and guide us through our own learning and healing, but they cannot do it for us. For no matter how much others may
love us and help us, they cannot heal our old wounds. These can be

healed only by learning to love ourselves and moving through our fear, grief, and pain.

Mothering

We are using the term *mothering* to connote an attitude and a way of being. It is something both men and women can do, but in our culture it has, unfortunately, been relegated primarily to women. This seems to be changing, however, as more men connect from their loving Adult to their Inner Child and discover their desire to love and nurture others.

Mothering is something we may need if we were not lovingly held by either of our parents, or something we need to help us feel safe enough to face deep trauma from our childhood. Sometimes the pain of the Inner Child is just so great that even our loving Inner Adult may need an extra loving adult around to hold us and help us through it.

Sometimes when we hurt or feel alone or afraid, we may fantasize the perfect Mom or Dad, someone who knows just how to comfort us. He or she gives us unconditional love and always knows the perfect thing to say. When we think of being mothered, we think of being held and allowed to be the small Child within us. Our mother or father, filled with compassion and forgiveness, is there to protect us and to see that we have a safe place in which to learn about and move through our pain. It is healing to be held, touched, and stroked.

When we think of mothering we usually think only of children. The truth is that we all, at times, need mothering, no matter how old we are. Many of us may be very good at giving nurturing and support to others, but may fail to realize that sometimes we need it ourselves. Men often get mothering from their spouse or girlfriend, but many women find themselves giving the nurturing to their husbands or lovers but not getting it back. Women, too, need the softness and kindness of mothering but often have difficulty getting that need met. Some men, those who show up as a loving Adult with their own Inner Child, are soft and tender and truly able to nurture and support, and the lucky women who are with them can get mothering when they need it. But men who have abandoned their Inner Child often just want to *be* mothered.

Many of the women we work with have ignored the need to be mothered or are completely unaware of it, because they see no way to get it met. They constantly press the men in their lives to provide this kind of tenderness, but are consistently unsuccessful. Sometimes women sexualize the need for mothering and attempt to get this need met through sex with their husbands or lovers. Other women may sexualize this need with women and decide erroneously that they are lesbians.

When we first presented the idea of mothering to one of our groups, some of the women were very opposed to the idea, expressing the belief that adults should outgrow the need for mothering in order to be truly adult. Some quickly understood the healing power of mothering and applied it to their lives. One woman was particularly touched by the subject. She was a very serious woman in her mid-thirties. She had been working on the issues of emptiness and aloneness and was dialoguing with her Inner Child, but found that sometimes she just wanted to be held. Her husband found it difficult to hold her without expecting sex. She didn't know how to get this need met and found herself pressuring her husband and daughter for approval instead. As we shared with her our own experiences of mothering and nurturing, her eyes filled with tears. She said that she had never been held by her mother when she was a child and had always wanted that kind of comfort but didn't know where to find it. The other women in the group were deeply moved by her openness and sadness. They encircled her, providing support and love as they held her. Within a few weeks she opened far more deeply to her Inner Child and discovered that her Child wanted more friends to play with. She made contact with her women friends and began spending time with them to explore herself and grow. She gave herself permission to be a little girl and to play and be held at times. She became more sensitive to the needs of her daughter and found herself more open and able to play with her. She learned to recognize her needs and meet them, rather than judge them. A short time later she announced in group that she felt it was time for her to "graduate." Mothering had been a core issue for her. She had been angry and unfulfilled trying to deny that her Inner Child wanted mothering. When she opened to the truth, the whole world opened to her. She stopped pressuring her family, and in turn she received more love as she herself became more loving. She no longer feared that she was being childish or immature if she needed to be held.

When we asked some of the women in our groups to share what mothering has meant to them, Kathy and Gwen decided to do it together on tape. The following is a transcription of their tape.

Kathy: I met Gwen in Margie and Erika's women's group. I was immediately attracted to her bright, pretty face and her wonderful laughter. I felt for probably the first time since junior high like a preteen girl wanting to connect and be friends with this person. I remember racing up to her after group, to find out whether she wanted to be friends with me.

Gwen: When I first met Kathy, I just about fell in love. She was so pretty, and her eyes were so bright and so full of fun. I knew I wanted to be her friend. I even started to have sexual fantasies about her. Margie suggested that I was sexualizing my need for mothering. I had no idea what she meant. *Mothering?* My mother was a cold and frightening bitch.

Kathy: *Mothering* is such a strange word. Whenever I hear it, images of my mother come to mind, when in fact true mothering as I've come to know it is often not at all what I experienced while growing up. So often when I was held or comforted by my mother, it didn't feel comforting at all, it felt smothering, as if she was using the opportunity to manipulate, fix, teach, or own me. This was so confusing! Here she was trying to "help" me, and after all, she was my mother; but the bottom line was that it didn't feel good to me. I could feel the walls come up inside of me.

Gwen: Two things were happening with my mother. One was that she couldn't acknowledge my pain, my insecurities, my fears, or my loneliness. The other was that she could barely stand to hold me. I used to watch some of the women hold each other in group. They were so sweet and soft and caring. It just about broke my heart, I wanted that so badly. I realized I needed to be held . . . a lot. It was hard for me to ask, but it made it so much easier for me to open to the feelings of my Inner Child when Kathy was holding me, soothing my pain and confusion in a sweet and caring way. Then I would hold Kathy when she cried.

Kathy: Having Gwen hold me was such a different experience. How wonderful it is to be held when I'm in pain and to be allowed to be with my feelings, to be accepted and loved for who I am and for whatever I'm feeling, with no expectations that I change or learn someone else's lesson—to be held by someone who is not uncomfortable with my pain. I experience true mothering when Gwen allows me to experience the feelings of my Inner Child and to heal myself. There is no "fixing" going on. A circle of energy is created that is healing and empowering.

Gwen: When Kathy mothers me, my Child feels safe and loved and protected. I open up and feel the incredible power of my own lovingness and ability to heal myself. When Kathy and I first became friends, we were playmates, almost like adolescents. We went to Disneyland without our kids so *we* could be the kids. We talked on the phone every night.

Kathy: What began as hours a day on the phone together, sharing secrets about ourselves, listening to and consoling each other for the other problems in our lives, has developed into a real connection, a path of personal growth together. Even at first, our conversations were never complaining sessions. We were there to listen and help each other learn from whatever situation we were dealing with. That's what has made this relationship so special. This is not about complaining or blaming the husband or the kid; it is about taking personal responsibility in realizing our own potential for happiness.

Gwen: Our relationship started as a playful, energetic connection. We could be kids together and care for each other unselfconsciously, like children. It moved into mothering, holding, caring, and soothing when the other was in pain, when the other's Child needed to be held.

Kathy: Our friendship has taken a lot of pressure off my relationship with my husband. I realized that all the things I was pressuring him for—connection, mutual growth, and fun—didn't have to all come from him. Just because he wasn't providing them all the time didn't mean that I couldn't have them when I needed them.

Gwen: We support each other in our inner work toward becoming happy, loving people. We support each other in healing our pain and developing our joy. We help each other with our own issues and explore the ones we trigger in each other. For me, believing that Kathy can love me without judgment, unconditionally, is probably one of the most significant events in my life. That's the real mothering, right there.

Kathy: It's important to me and for me to remember what "mothering" has come to mean to me when I'm dealing with my own twelve-year-old daughter—to know that this is what she needs, too. I know that, given unconditional love and trust, she will find her own answers.

What is exciting for me at this point in our relationship is that we have an arena in which to work on the core beliefs of our egos, the erroneous beliefs that have gotten in the way of our growth and happiness all our lives. Sometimes, one of us will touch off one of these beliefs in the other. I think this is a good time to talk about some of these issues that come up between us. One of the really important ones has to do with our own mothers. With me, it's "Oh God, I'm going to be swallowed up." And when Gwen holds me, I'm terrified that it's my "old" mom, not my "new" mom (laughter).

Gwen: One of my issues is the fear that I'm unlovable, that I'm disgusting and no one could possibly stand me. If that fear arises when I'm with Kathy, during a loving circle, I can deal with it then—it ceases to be threatening.

Kathy: If it weren't for Gwen, I would have no one with whom to work on these issues—no one who would touch them off or help me recognize them. We work these things through together because they get in our way.

Gwen: It's so funny. It used to be that things would get in the way with other people in our lives and we'd work through those issues. Now, we actually work on the issues that get in the way of our own relationship. This kind of relationship magnifies the issues. When we're this close and we're so willing to work, we see how powerful even the smallest problems are; we see their potential for undermining our happiness.

Kathy: Right. I just want to add that this is a really exciting part of our relationship to me, because these old, old issues have usually gotten in the way a lot in my life. When they come up between us, it's a chance to really look at them and learn from them and finally get past them.

Cheryl's mother died when Cheryl was ten years old. Cheryl wrote the following about her experience with mothering.

I had always felt ambivalent about touching and hugging. I wanted the experience and yet I just could not totally accept it. I would see parents, mothers in particular, holding their children's hands, and I would feel anger and longing at the same time. I also still had a great longing for my mother, even though it had been thirty years since she died. I never connected either of these feelings with a strong need for mothering until one night at group therapy when we were talking about mothering. Erika mentioned how she and her friends provide one another with mothering. At first it seemed strange that a woman would still want and need that. At the same time, I realized that I was hungry for that contact too. That whole aspect of my life vanished when my mother died and my father subsequently married two abusive women. After a while I refused to acknowledge that need. It was almost as if I decided that they couldn't hurt me if I didn't need them. So I didn't know that the little girl in me still needed mothering.

When Erika glanced over at me and touched my hand, it seemed as if she knew what I was thinking and that it was okay. At that point I chose to go with my feelings because I felt safe, so I crawled into her arms. Suddenly, the pain from all the years of denial welled up, and I started to cry. As I was crying, I realized that the denial had caused me more pain than reaching out could have.

Charles came to therapy for help with his addiction to sex. Whenever he felt anxious, he would seek sex with his wife. If she wasn't available, he would go to porno shops and occasionally have sex with other women. During therapy, Charles remembered being molested by his mother and realized that she had never held him in a nonsexual way. For him love, approval, and sex had become one, so whenever he felt alone, he would use sex to feel better. Charles's wife, Abby, was struggling with her own feelings of aloneness and her memories of never having been held lovingly by her mother. As both Charles and Abby recognized their need for mothering and began to spend more time just holding each other and talking, instead of always having sex, Charles's sexual obsession slowly melted away.

William came to therapy for help with his sexual identity. He was attracted to men but wanted to marry and have a family. He liked women but felt no sexual attraction to them. As he began to remember his childhood, he realized that he had been raised by an extremely cold and controlling mother, who was also covertly seductive. William's father, a soft and caring man, had died when William was five, and William was left at the mercy of his mother. William realized that suppressing his sexual response to women was the only way he had known to protect himself from being totally controlled by his mother.

William has accepted mothering from the therapist and is seeking mothering from other women as well. As this process heals his fear of women, he will be able to choose to be homosexual, bisexual, or heterosexual. If he chooses homosexuality, it will be because that's where his happiness lies and not because he is afraid of women.

Just as women need mothering from other women, so men need mothering from other men. Few men were held enough by their fathers, so most men need affection and support from other men. Yet there are even more taboos on men holding men than there are on women holding women. It is so sad that our culture so often sexualizes a need for holding, touching, comfort, affection, and support.

Touching

Some people are afraid of touching or of being touched. They perceive touching as a demand for something. To them touching has become associated with giving themselves up, with giving in and having sex, or with suppressing their feelings.

There are many kinds of touches, and many of them do not feel good or comforting. If touching is offered with the intention to give love, then it is easy to accept and it feels healing. If the touch is seductive and sexual, it may not be welcome. You can touch someone from your Higher Self, intending to give something, or you can touch someone from your ego, intending to get something.

Touch from the Ego

The Seductive Touch

The seductive touch says, "I want affirmation from you through sexuality. I am not touching you to give you love, but rather to get something from you—your sexual response. When you respond to me sexually, then I will know I am okay." Parents who touch their children seductively create enormous problems for them. The child is caught between a desire for the parent's love and fear of violation. As a result, many children shut off their responses altogether, to protect themselves from the violation they fear.

Adults generally feel violated as well when the intention of the touch is to seek sex rather than give love. This, as we said earlier, is crazy-making, especially when the person touching insists that he or she is just being loving. The touch doesn't feel good, yet the other person often denies his or her intention. Many of the people we have worked with complain that the only time their husbands or wives are affectionate is when they want sex. They say that that kind of affection doesn't feel good; it feels manipulative.

The Smothering Touch

Some people touch and hold others in order to control them and get their attention, love, or affection, just as one holds a small, squirming puppy. The person's needs come before the puppy's happiness. This often happens with small children, and the results are disastrous. A women named Lynn in one of our groups was overtly afraid of being touched, especially by women. As we explored this issue, she said she felt that to be touched was life-threatening, that somehow she would not only lose her individuality but her life as well. She allowed us to hold her, and as we did, she began to remember her mother. She recalled with great detail how her mother would smother her in her arms. Her mother would say over and over, "But I love you" to her wriggling child. Little Lynn didn't feel loved; she felt trapped and used. As a result she couldn't allow herself to be touched or to enjoy closeness.

The smothering touch says, "You are not a free individual. Your body is my property. Therefore, I have the right to hold you, touch you, or pinch you whenever I want. Your purpose is to give me love, to make me feel okay. I don't care what you want, but it is your job to care about what I want. I have a right to impose myself on you, and if you love me you will let me control you this way." People who smother others with their touch like to think of themselves as very loving people, never realizing that they are violating the other person's boundaries.

Margie remembered an experience like that.

I was once giving a talk to a group of ministers. After the talk many of the ministers came up to hug me in a caring way and tell me how much they enjoyed the talk. One of the men, however, wrapped his arms around me and kept me there. When I tried to pull away, he tightened his arms. The message was, "If you pull away, I will feel insulted." Of course, his hug did not feel loving. When I finally managed to extricate myself from his grasp, he looked at me with a broad self-satisfied grin, convinced that he was the most loving man there.

The Placating Touch

The placating touch says, "There, there, don't feel bad. Stop hurting, because I can't handle your pain." Parents often touch or hold children this way, rather than simply comforting them while they experience their pain. They give their children the message that if they are being held, then they shouldn't feel pain anymore. This is a confusing double message. The overt message is "I love you." The covert message is "My love is conditional on your putting a lid on your pain." This feels manipulative and bad to the child. Parents who believe they are bad parents when their child is in pain will try to get the child to stop crying so that they, the parents, don't have to feel bad. Or, if the child's pain triggers the parents' own childhood pain and the parents will not face it, the parents will do anything to cut off their child's pain, including emotional and physical abuse.

Partners will often use this touch with each other, patting the other person in an attempt to appear nice, but really saying "Don't be upset (or don't cry), because I can't handle it." The placating touch feels patronizing rather than comforting.

The Nondemanding Touch from the Higher Self

The nondemanding touch is the essence of true mothering. It is an unconditionally loving touch that says, "I am here for you. I am with you in your sadness, your fear, your grief, your terror, your agony, your pain, your joy. I have no expectations that you need to meet. I love you just as you are, and I am here for you however you choose to be." This touch gives comfort; it is filled with love and tenderness. It is a healing touch.

It is this unconditionally loving touch that can help to heal the desperate loneliness and aloneness of the Inner Child. This pain, so hard to feel, can be experienced in the presence of another loving person, so that we don't have to feel alone in experiencing the old pain of our abandoned Child. Erika describes her experience as a therapist using the nondemanding touch.

Traditional therapies dictate that you never touch your clients, for all kinds of unpleasant and unproven reasons: it may be interpreted as sexual, or the client may become too dependent, or it may cause transference problems. I don't believe I have ever worked with a client whom I haven't held like a child or touched. Often people have difficulty connecting with their Inner Child and articulating their feelings, and they need time to just feel. My holding them allows them to simply experience their feelings; it also creates an additional way in which to communicate. I can feel their energy and they can feel mine. If they are facing very painful issues, my holding them allows them to move through the pain safely. Men, women, and adolescents respond to love and kindness. It has never been my experience that clients become lazy and dependent, or use my holding them as a band-aid. On the contrary, I have found that the safer an environment I provide, the more likely it is that a person will address difficult issues and heal them. They seem to do this more quickly than those who must walk that path alone, without the love and mothering of someone else.

Open and Closed Pain

We do not automatically want to hold every person we see who is in tears. Our desire to hold another depends on the intent of the pain. There are two kinds of pain: open pain and closed pain. Open pain is the pain of loss and mourning and the acceptance of wounds. It is the pain we feel when we open to learning from our Inner Child. It is a healing pain that leads to understanding and choice. Closed pain is the pain of abandonment that occurs when we disconnect from our Inner Child and become a victim of our own choices. It is the "poor me," "I am a victim" pain that people use to manipulate others into taking care of them when they have chosen not to take care of themselves.

When we experience someone in open pain, we are moved by them. They are open to their own experience and blame no one for it. They just want to feel safe to move through the pain. To these people we almost always reach out and offer comfort. People in closed pain are quite different. Their tears don't move us, and we feel manipulated by them. If ever you are with someone in tears and you yourself are not touched, it's likely that they have chosen to protect themselves and have abdicated their Adult responsibility. They want someone else to take away their pain. They don't wish to learn; they want to be rescued. Holding a victim does not further their growth or help to heal their Inner Child; instead it fosters their addictions by teaching them that being a victim will get them what they want, at least for the moment.

Not everyone responds positively to a loving touch. It makes some people feel too vulnerable: they fear needing it too much, or they fear losing something that feels so good and that they have wanted for so long. For those who had little love in their lives as children, unconditional love can feel overwhelming. But unconditional love is so healing that eventually most people open to it.

There will be times in your life when you feel very motherly toward someone. There will also be times when you really want to be mothered and held. You will never fulfill your life and your needs without taking the risk to ask for and give what you want. We hope you will give yourself permission to hug, hold, and love, for this is what your Inner Child wants and deserves.

CHAPTER 11

Twelve-Step Programs

> To the general hopelessness of addiction, the Twelve Steps of recovery bring an elegant simplicity. The principles in them may well be universal. They were not original with A.A., but have been found in every major religion and philosophy.
>
> *Sex and Love Addicts Anonymous*
> THE AUGUSTINE FELLOWSHIP

The Twelve-Step programs consist of men and women who, as the Alcoholics Anonymous Big Book states, gather together to "share their experience, strength, and hope with each other that they may solve their common problem and help others recover from alcoholism"—or any other addiction. Involvement in a Twelve-Step program is often an essential part of an individual's recovery. Overcoming addictions is a very difficult process; the Twelve-Step programs provide an invaluable framework within which to learn, as well as the often necessary support and sense of community. People often feel completely alone with their struggles, but with Twelve-Step programs so available, one never needs to be alone. It's incredibly helpful to hear other people talk openly about things that you may have kept secret your whole life. In Twelve-Step programs you meet people in various stages of recovery, and you can learn and heal as each person shares his or her pain and growth. In addition, it is often a place to meet like-minded people, people who want to grow and are dedicated to their recovery. It is important, when you first decide to start attending a Twelve-Step program, to find a meeting where you feel comfortable. Not all meetings are the same, and it is important to find people you can relate to.

Twelve-Step programs are available for almost every form of substance and process addiction. They include Alcoholics Anonymous, Narcotics Anonymous, Cocaine Anonymous, Overeaters Anonymous, Smokers Anonymous, Debtors Anonymous, Sexaholics Anonymous, Sex Addicts Anonymous, Sexual Compulsives Anonymous, and Sex and Love Addicts Anonymous. While Twelve-Step programs are most noted for their work with substance abuse, they work equally well with approval, love, sex, and romance addicts. In addition, there are Twelve-Step programs for helping those who have been involved with substance and process addicts: Adult Children of Alcoholics (ACoA), Al-Anon and Alateen for mates and teenagers of alcoholics, Incest Survivors Anonymous, and Codependents of Sex Addicts (COSA).

If you don't identify with any of the above but know that something is not right in your relationships, try Codependents Anonymous (CoDA). In our experience, codependency is the underlying issue in all addictive behavior. If you are a member of any of the above Twelve-Step programs, you might eventually want to add CoDA to your list of preferred meetings. All Twelve-Step program groups are free and open to anyone.

Very often, when we refer a client to a Twelve-Step program, we run into a lot of resistance. The resistance usually falls into three categories: 1. I don't want to mix with a bunch of losers; 2. I can't get into that God, Higher Power spiritual stuff; or 3. I can do it myself. What we've said in response to the first objection is, "Yes, some of the people in these programs are losers, but certainly not all of them, or even most of them. There are people from all walks of life in Twelve-Step programs. Try different meetings until you find people whom you relate to, whom you admire and respect. They are out there."

What we've said in response to the second objection is, "You can see God or a Higher Power any way you want. It doesn't have to be a source outside of yourself. The Higher Power can be your own Higher Self." We have found that as people become aware of and develop their own Higher Self, they naturally move into experiencing the universal love that is the true source of healing, particularly in healing their aloneness. The more we face the aloneness of our Inner Child with our own loving Adult, the more we experience that we are truly not alone.

What we've said in response to the third objection is, "No, you can't do it alone, or you already would have. One of the lies the ego tells us to maintain control over us is that we can do it ourselves, or that we should be able to do it ourselves. No one heals by himself or herself."

Each group adapts the Twelve Steps to fit its particular program. Below are the twelve steps we offer for use in any of the programs:

1. Admitted that in our ego state—unloving Adult and abandoned Child—we are powerless over our addictions, that our lives had become unmanageable.

2. Came to believe that giving up ego control, surrendering to our Higher Self/Higher Power, and learning from our Higher Self how to be a loving Adult for our Inner Child could restore us to sanity.

3. Made a decision to turn our lives over to our Higher Selves by learning with our Inner Child.

4. Made an honest assessment of the ways we have chosen to protect ourselves and of the beliefs and unhealed wounds behind those defenses.

5. Admitted to our Higher Power, ourselves, and at least one other person the whole story of our self-protections, wounds, and beliefs that caused us to abandon our Inner Child.

6. Decided to open to our Higher Power/Higher Selves and relinquish the protections of the ego by assuming responsibility for our own Inner Child.

7. Surrendered our ego control and lovingly sought guidance from our Higher Power in meeting the needs and feelings of our Inner Child.

8. Made a list of all the ways we had harmed our Inner Child and others and became willing to make amends.

9. Began the process of forgiving ourselves and making amends to our Inner Child and to others we had harmed, except when doing so would be unloving.

10. Continued to pay close attention to the needs and feelings of our Inner Child and to take prompt action to reconnect when we disconnect.

11. Sought through meditation and written and oral dialogue to improve our connection to ourselves, to others, and to the universe.

12. Having had a spiritual awakening as a result of these steps, we reached out to others with love and caring.

It is impossible to even begin to connect with your Inner Child if you are a practicing alcoholic or a drug addict. We call these substances "ego foods," since they keep you in your ego and prevent you from connecting to your self. Dialoguing or even being in therapy will get you nowhere until you abstain, and most people cannot do this by themselves. We do not accept for therapy practicing alcoholics or drug addicts until they commit to a Twelve-Step program. Unless they are in a Twelve-Step program, therapy is a waste of time.

We strongly encourage you to avail yourselves of the support and learning provided by the Twelve-Step programs.

CHAPTER 12

Processes in Therapy

The opportunity to be part of . . . healing feels a little like assisting at a birth. It's awesome to touch the miracle of life so closely.
The Courage to Heal
ELLEN BASS AND LAURA DAVIS

It is very helpful to work with a therapist who can assist you in learning what it means to be a loving Adult to your Inner Child, who can support you as you face your pain and grief, and who can help you explore the false beliefs that keep you stuck in your fear and pain. No therapist, no matter how skilled, can do the work for you, but a competent therapist can be invaluable in helping you learn how to heal your own pain. Too often, however, people come into therapy hoping the therapist is some sort of magician and can heal them without their having to do their own work. This stems from the basic belief that other people can make you happy, the belief that if only the therapist is loving enough and accepting enough, then you will feel good about yourself and be healed. A good therapist provides mothering when needed and is nonjudgmental and open to learning, but the therapist offers the truth as he or she sees it, told with compassion, rather than blanket approval.

Individual Therapy

Many people do not feel safe in therapy, not necessarily because the therapist is judgmental, but because the Inner Adult has abandoned the Inner Child, who then needs the approval of the therapist to feel okay. When clients want approval rather than truth, they will not feel safe with therapists who are not codependent and who do not foster their clients' codependence. Codependent therapists give sympathy and approval in the hopes of gaining their clients' approval. They fear that if they speak the truth as they experience it their clients will get mad at them. Speaking the truth might mean saying to a client, "I experience you as blaming your husband for your pain rather than facing the pain of your own choices," instead of merely sympathizing. If clients really want to learn, they will appreciate such insights, but if they just want to be told they are right and gain sympathy or approval, they will feel unsafe and may leave to search for a more sympathetic therapist. It is unloving for a therapist to feed a client's addiction to approval. This is not to say that the therapist should withhold approval, but that he or she should not use approval as a way to foster the client's addiction to the therapist.

A therapist's job is to help a client understand how to take personal responsibility for his or her own pain and joy. This means helping the client learn how to truly love the Inner Child by learning how to accept the Child's old pain and grief, how to explore the false beliefs causing the pain, and how to listen to the Inner Child and act in behalf of the Child's wants and needs. The therapist can provide a role model for loving behavior by demonstrating an intent to learn, and by helping the client become aware of his or her unloving, authoritarian, or permissive self-parenting. The therapist can provide further help by role-playing the client's loving Adult when the client is being the Inner Child, particularly when the client's Inner Child is feeling abandoned, or by role-playing the client's Inner Child and letting the client practice being loving or become aware of how he or she is being unloving. We call this therapy *Inner Bonding Therapy*.

The therapist can provide loving support to assist the client in feeling anger and pain. When deep childhood memories come up and the fear and pain is intense, the therapist can provide mothering, if this is what the client needs, to help the client move through it. Memories of emotional, physical, and sexual abuse are extremely difficult to feel; it is very helpful to have a loving therapist providing a safe environment in which to experience and move through these deep feelings.

It is extremely important for the therapist to help the client learn to do his or her own work. Too often, clients become dependent on the therapist and do not continue to do their learning by themselves during the week. Seeing a therapist once or twice a week is not enough to heal. You must be willing to continue to work with your Inner Child every day on your own. One reason why people end up in therapy for so long is that the only time they do their work is in the therapist's office, and they never really get anywhere that way. Long-term therapy may actually become another addiction.

Below is an example of a session where the client, Jessica, is doing much of her own work, with some help from the therapist.

Jessica: I went down to see my two brothers who both live in the San Diego area. I stayed with my older brother, Richard, and his girlfriend, Margo. She's a really remarkable lady. She is considerably older than he is—he's thirty-seven and she's probably fifty. She is this little, gentle lady with white-blonde hair, and she's really cool. I love her, and I love my brother. At one point I went into their bedroom because I needed to ask them a question. They were in bed together, and this feeling of revulsion to the point of nausea came over me—and these are two people whom I love and whose relationship I think is really good and healthy. I want to keep working on the issue of sex until this sort of thing goes away. So when I ask myself what that was all about, it comes down to the fact that Richard doesn't want to marry her. She can't have children, and he says he wants to have children eventually. So I think the revulsion was about . . . I'm not really sure. It may have to do with beliefs left over from when I was really young (that are obviously still present now) that a woman shouldn't do that kind of thing unless she is married. And I guess I feel that if a woman sleeps with a man and she is not married to him, she is really being *stupid*. God, I'm nervous. I'm nervous talking about this. But this is all head stuff. I'm not getting down into my belly yet.

Therapist: Why don't you ask your Child what she feels about it?

Jessica: Oh. (speaks to the doll) What was going on with us when that happened? (She shifts to the chair with the doll, holds the doll, and speaks in a little girl's voice.)

Jessica's Child: We shouldn't have been there. We shouldn't have been there at all. We shouldn't have gone into that room at all. That was their private place, and we shouldn't have been there at all. I wish we hadn't seen them like that. (She starts to cry.) I didn't want to see them like that at all. I didn't want to see them like that. It was a bad thing to do. We shouldn't have gone in there.

Jessica's Adult: Why do you think it was a bad thing to do? They invited us in. They said it was okay.

Jessica's Child: But it wasn't. It wasn't okay. They weren't dressed. *They weren't dressed.* And it was *icky*!

Jessica's Adult: So you think they shouldn't have invited us in? Because they weren't dressed? (to the therapist) God, I don't know where this is going . . .

Therapist: Ask her if it reminds her of anything that happened to you as a little girl.

Jessica: Okay. Does it remind you of anything that happened to you when we were really little?

Jessica's Child: Well, all I can think of is I saw Daddy in the bathroom once, but that's not it. Huh uh. (pause) I remember going to Mom and Dad's bedroom once and knocking on the door because there were funny noises coming out, but it was locked . . . (longer pause)

Jessica's Adult: Why do you think it was wrong?

Jessica's Child: (upset now) Because I didn't want to go in. Because I didn't want to see anything. I don't want to look at them. I don't want to see them. I don't want to look at that kind of stuff. I don't want to see Richard doing that kind of stuff. It makes me sick.

Jessica's Adult: Why does it make you sick to see . . . Oh, now we're getting to it—

Jessica's Child: (crying) Because he's not married to her and he's doing the same kind of thing that Daddy did. I don't want Richard to be like Daddy. I don't want him to be like Daddy. He's *not* like Daddy. *No. I don't want him to be!*

Jessica's Adult: Why do you think Rich is like Daddy? He doesn't treat Margo like Daddy treated Mommy, does he?

Jessica's Child: No . . . but in a way he does, because he doesn't love her enough to marry her and . . . there's a part of him that thinks she's too old, or not pretty enough or not smart enough or something, and that's the same thing that Dad did to Mom. It's the *same* thing. It's that "She's not good enough" *shit*. And that's what he does to *her*. Because he won't marry her. He doesn't really love her. He thinks he's God's gift to women. He's just as arrogant as Daddy was. And it makes me *sick*. Because I don't want him to be like Daddy was (to the therapist, still crying). That's the bottom line.

Therapist: So it seems like the nausea was a projection onto Rich of the really deep feelings that your Child has about your father.

Jessica: Yeah, very much so.

Therapist: Do you want to give your little girl a voice right now and try to talk to your father and express your revulsion?

Jessica: Yeah. Yeah.

Therapist: Put your father over there.

Jessica's Child: You're awful. You're so mean to Mom. (crying) You're so mean to her. And you're so mean to Donnie. And I don't trust you at all. You treat Momma bad. You treat yourself bad. You blame everybody and you're mean and you hate everybody.

Therapist: Wasn't the revulsion about sexuality?

Jessica's Child: (crying again) Yeah. Yeah. I think you screwed every waitress in the restaurant. [Her father owned a restaurant.]

Therapist: How about your revulsion?

Jessica's Child: And it makes me *sick*!!! It makes me get sick to my stomach! And it makes me want to kick you and hit you and cut off your penis and put it through a meat grinder and hit you and poke your eyes in and pull your tongue out and chop your lips off and kick you in the face and hit you in the stomach. And it makes me want to throw up all over you too! And I feel sorry for anybody you took in!!! And I'm mad at Mom for sticking around you too. And the time when you came back after you were up in San Francisco and . . . and you two . . .

you went into the bedroom for hours, and she came out and she couldn't even *walk* straight . . . that made me *sick* too. It made me *sick*!!! 'Cause your marriage was in such trouble and you guys didn't talk at all, you just went in the bedroom and *screwed*, you never talked. And she let it happen! It made me sick!!! It made me sick!!! I hated you!

Therapist: Do you want to put your Mom over there?

Jessica's Child: You make me sick, too! You never stand up for yourself! You never say no to him! You never tell him to just *fuck off*!!! You never told him what you knew and you never told him to *stop it* and you never told him how much it *hurt* you! And you let him run all over you and use you like a doormat! He wiped his feet all over you! And you just pretended that nothing was wrong . . . (long pause) I wish you had just kicked him out. I wish you had just told him to go to hell and moved us all away from him. You were nice and he was a mean son-of-a-bitch! And I wish you'd had a job so we could have done that. And I wish I'd told you that, too.

Therapist: Is there anything else you want to tell them?

Jessica's Child: Yeah, the two of you were *awful* together. You never should have married. Mom, you shouldn't have let him put you down so much. You didn't deserve it. And Dad, you're an arrogant son-of-a-bitch, and just because her hearing wasn't very good you shouldn't have done what you did to her. She was a nice lady and that was her main flaw. She was too nice to *you*. I think you needed somebody to fight with. I wish you'd gotten a divorce when I was about *two*!!! I just wish you'd both been happy, but you were both miserable. (pause, then fresh tears) And there is one other thing I want to say to my little brother Donnie. I'm *real sorry*, Donnie, that it happened to you, too, that Daddy was so mean to you, too, and that I didn't say anything to him or tell him to *shut up*. I'm really sorry, I'm *really really really sorry*, Donnie. I'm really sorry. (long pause) I'm sorry because of Mom, and I'm sorry because of you. I'm sorry I didn't tell Daddy the truth for you, too. And I'm sorry I didn't tell the truth for me, too.

Therapist: Are you angry at your Adult for not giving you a voice? For not allowing you to say your truth?

Jessica: No, because I think he would have beat us up if we'd have said anything when he was that angry. I don't think we could have said anything. And he never hit us, but I think it's because we really were careful around him. And I think if we'd pushed him any further, something awful could have happened. But I guess you're right—I think I'm mad at me, 'cause I wish we'd at least tried. We could have tried and run away. We could have tried something else. I'm sorry we didn't try something else. But I'm not really angry, I'm just sorry we didn't try something else. (pause) I'm still mad at my Dad. I'm still mad at him. I'm not so mad at my Mom, but I'm still mad at him. (long pause) I'm still really mad at him for screwing all the waitresses at the restaurant. In a funny way, it feels like he hurt me directly by doing that. You know, I felt like we weren't enough for him, and *I wasn't enough for him.* I guess the basic belief is he screwed the waitresses because we weren't enough for him, and that meant that I wasn't enough for him.

Therapist: Why don't you tell your little girl about that now.

Jessica's Adult: Oh. (to her Child, in a whisper) It isn't that you weren't enough for him. That isn't it at all. It isn't that you weren't *enough* . . . You might not have been . . . you probably weren't enough for him. I don't know what he was looking for; he never found it. But that doesn't mean that you weren't *enough.* You're fine. You're wonderful. And you know what? I think Daddy would be awful upset if he knew what we've made of his actions. I don't think this is what he wanted us to feel at all. But the bottom line is that it's not that you're not enough. You're just wonderful. (starts to cry, the weak comforting the weak) You're a beautiful little girl. And you care about people, and you're funny and sweet, and you try to give as much as you can, and you make people laugh and smile. You're a wonderful little girl. You're a *wonderful* little girl. It wasn't your fault that Dad did all that. It wasn't your fault. It wasn't your fault that Daddy did all those things. It wasn't your fault . . .

Therapist: Jessica, I want you to try to tell her from a more Adult place. I don't know if she can hear you and believe you from the place you're in right now.

Jessica's Adult: (regroups, stops crying) You know, it wasn't your fault.

Therapist: See if you can come from a place of conviction and power.

Jessica's Adult: And not from the weakness and the vulnerability. Okay. (to the Child, voice firmer, like an Adult trying to reason a child out of its feelings) You know, it wasn't your fault. It wasn't your fault that Daddy did what he did. You actually had nothing to do with what he chose to do. You had nothing to do with it. (to the therapist) Boy, I don't believe that myself.

Therapist: That's why you were telling it to her from the abandoned place. When you can tell it to her from a place of Adult truth and conviction, then she's going to start to feel it. She won't *feel* it until you know that truth.

Jessica: See, what's true for me is if I had been more honest, if I had given him my truth . . . I feel as if I did contribute to what he chose to do because I added to the dishonesty.

Therapist: You're coming from a false belief.

Jessica: Good. What is it?

Therapist: That there was anything that you could say or do that would have made a difference.

Jessica: That's the same thing I came up against with Jack [her employer].

Therapist: Yes. It's a control issue. You think if you had been more honest, if you had said your truth, that you could have made a difference. The only difference it would have made was to you. It would have made a difference internally to your Inner Child to have a voice. But it wouldn't have made any difference in what he did. Because someone else's truth is not what changes people. It's only their truth that changes them.

Jessica's Adult: Yeah. (to the Child, trying again) We had no power over him. We had *no magical power* over him. (Something has shifted inside, she sounds certain and comforting at last.) No matter how honest we were, and no matter how much we loved him, we had no magical power to change his brain or to change his heart. We couldn't do it. *We couldn't do it.* We did our very best. We did our very best to love. We did our very best to be a good girl, and we did our very best to be happy around him and Mom, and we did our very best to make them happy, too. And you know what? We didn't have that power! We didn't.

Therapist: Not only that, but you have no way of knowing what would have happened if you had said your truth. He might have even been worse!

Jessica's Adult: That's right! If we had said our truth, it might have been worse.

Therapist: We learned not to tell our truth as children because often it made things worse, not better.

Jessica's Adult: (to her Child) See, if Daddy had really wanted to make changes in his life, he would have been looking for the truth. He would have been looking for other ways to be. He would have been searching inside of himself, he would have been talking with other people about how to be different, he would have maybe been seeing a psychologist, he would have been doing all sorts of things differently. But those were his choices. You see, he had the power, he had the money, he had the time, he had the ability to make those choices, and for whatever reason, he didn't. And that wasn't our fault. We did our very best. What we have to do now is kind of let Daddy go and . . . and whatever he's earned and whatever challenges he's facing now, we have to just let those go for him, that's what he has to face and we need to let go of that. We just need to know that we did our very best. We have no magic power to change people. The only magical power we have is to change ourselves, to talk like this and change ourselves. *That's* our magic power! That's our magic power. And I love you. (to the therapist) That feels good. That magic power . . . I guess I've never given up, until now, the belief that I did have that magic power. Feels like a lot of stuff just released on that. I don't feel angry at him for screwing waitresses anymore.

Therapist: That was good work.

Jessica: Thank you.

Working with Specific Disorders

Some disorders are quite resistant to help through therapy. Often people suffering from them go from therapist to therapist without progress. We will discuss a number of these disorders here and show how healing can occur through Inner Bonding Therapy. But we wish to state again that no disorder can be healed unless the client is *willing* to do the inner work.

Personality Disorders

Unfortunately, personality disorders are quite common and cause moderate to severe social, occupational, and relationship impairment. According to the *Diagnostic and Statistical Manual of Mental Disorders (DSM-111-R)*, published by the American Psychiatric Association, the most common personality disorders are borderline, histrionic, narcissistic, avoidant, dependent, and obsessive-compulsive disorders.

Our experience with clients suffering from personality disorders is that their root is a deep and consistent disconnection between the Inner Adult and the Inner Child. These people have either an extremely rigid authoritarian Adult who runs things and completely excludes the Child, as in obsessive-compulsive personality disorder. Or, more commonly, they have an extremely permissive Adult who is basically nonexistent and the abandoned Child is left completely alone to handle things, as in borderline, histrionic, narcissistic, avoidant, and dependent personality disorders.

Because the disconnection is so profound, healing takes much longer than it does for those people whose Adult and Child connect in some areas. In many people the Adult abandons the Child only when certain issues are activated, but personality disorders represent an across-the-board disconnection, which is why these people have such a hard time in both their work and their relationships.

Personality disorders are difficult to treat because it is hard to contact the Adult at all, and the Adult must be willing to learn. But we have found that if a client will commit to oral and written dialogue for at least a half hour daily, progress can be made. The Child cannot help but begin to feel better and to heal through the dialoguing. If the client refuses to make that commitment, then no progress can be made unless the client comes for therapy at least three times a week and dialogues out loud in the therapist's office, with the therapist role-modeling the loving Inner Adult, as well as role-playing the abandoned Child.

Eating Disorders

Eating disorders such as anorexia nervosa, bulimia, and obesity are quite common in our culture and are showing up more and more in therapists' offices. A person with anorexia is generally an adolescent or young woman whose Adult and Child are very disconnected and whose Child has chosen to deal with an intense fear of loss of control by stringently controlling food intake. This Child, frightened of being controlled by others because of the severe abandonment by the Adult, chooses to control in an area where no one else can have control. No one can make her eat unless they hospitalize her and force-feed her. In such cases, the Adult may allow the Child to starve to death rather than show up and take responsibility.

Young women suffering from bulimia suffer a similar inner disconnection. In this case, the Child has learned to fill with food the intense inner aloneness that occurs when the Adult disconnects or when loneliness is activated through disconnected interaction with others. Eating becomes a way the Child learns to nurture herself when she experiences no inner nurturing from the Adult. Eating may become a way she responds when she feels out of control in the world. Food takes the edge off feeling out of control of how others treat her or feeling alone. So the Child eats and eats in her attempt to fill the vast inner void and take away the pain. When she is so full that she cannot eat any more and the yearning for nurturing is temporarily filled, her fear of rejection from being fat emerges and she purges herself with self-induced vomiting or laxatives or diuretics. She vacillates back and forth between bingeing and purging and dieting or fasting depending on whether the emptiness or the fears of rejection predominate.

Tamira is a beautiful young woman in her mid-twenties, intelligent and talented, a successful artist. She has suffered from bulimia since she was seventeen, when she discovered that it was easy for her to vomit. Before entering therapy, she had been working hard on her recovery through Overeaters Anonymous and had obtained some degree of abstinence, but was dismayed that it was still such a struggle for her.

Soon after entering therapy she began to work diligently with her Inner Child. At first her Child was silent with her, but she kept at it until her Child spoke up, and when she did, she spoke volumes.

Tamira was amazed at the information her Inner Child had for her. Her Child told her that when her Adult refused to hear her and act in her behalf, her Child felt so alone that she would eat to fill the emptiness. Tamira found her bingeing and purging episodes becoming less and less frequent as she stayed more and more connected to her Inner Child. As with all difficulties, the bulimia was but a symptom of the inner disconnection.

As Tamira's Inner Child became more and more accessible, Tamira learned that she had felt very lonely as a child. She had experienced her mother as cold and distant, and her Inner Child had a great need for mothering, which she had often filled with food. As Tamira reached out to friends to get her need for mothering met, she started to feel more in control of the bulimia. Then she became aware of how rejected she had always felt by her father, who had left when she was young, and how this had affected all her relationships with men. At this point she had the following written dialogue with her Child:

Tamira's Adult: Hi, little one.

Tamira's Child: Mom, I'm mad.

Tamira's Adult: Tell me why.

Tamira's Child: Those feelings about men made me feel so wriggly in my skin. I feel hugely uncomfortable. I want to get out—I was screaming inside all day. I hate this. It hurts so bad. I wanted to be God so badly. I want to eat all this food and never put on weight. I want all the laws of a practical universe not to apply to me. [desire for control] I feel so uncomfortable—I want to throw up or kill someone or rip my guts out. Mom, I want to die.

Tamira's Adult: Why, sweetheart?

Tamira's Child: Because nobody cares. Nobody loves me. I'm all alone. I feel so alone. I couldn't fulfill any of his [her father's] needs—so he just left me. Everything we had was so special to me. Obviously it didn't mean anything to him—he threw me out. But if it was his war with Mama, why did I get roped in? What part am I responsible for? What did I do?

Tamira's Adult: Sweetheart, you didn't do anything. It had nothing to do with you (telling her Child the truth).

Tamira's Child: But then why did he leave me? I loved him so much. He was my provider. He bought me ice cream and showed me off in public. He was proud of me with other people. Strange, not with me alone, just with his friends. Why, Mom?

Tamira's Adult: He did love you. He was just too scared to take care of you by himself. He knew he couldn't control his drinking and felt so ashamed of his behavior. He felt like you could see straight through to his soul, that he couldn't hide the truth of who he was from you.

Tamira's Child: But I could, that's why I loved him.

Tamira's Adult: I know, little one. That was the irony. He thought you only loved him because you were too young to know him. If he had only known . . . You've always done the very thing he's feared the most. You've always been here to help him cleanse his shame. You couldn't do it then—you didn't have the tools. You didn't fail— he couldn't hear you. He knew it wasn't time. He couldn't handle it even though the answer was right in front of him. He discounted the gift you offered with your loving gaze. He didn't feel worthy of your adoration, your innocent trust and unconditional love and devotion.

Tamira's Child: Mom, do all men leave you when you show them how much love you have inside? Is it ugly?

Tamira's Adult: No, sweetheart. Only the men who don't love themselves enough to accept your gift. Your heart is so big that we haven't yet found a guy who can deal with the enormity of your beauty. When you love them and they can't love back, they feel shame. It is their shame which makes them run away. Not you, darling.

Tamira's Child: Mom, thank you. It feels so good to cry. Will you help me find men friends with whom I don't feel I have to

compromise myself and who won't restrict me and
make me conform to their needs? I want to be loved
for being 100 percent *me*.

Tamira's Adult: You are totally lovable and that is a promise. I'll listen
to you when I'm with guys, and you tell me what you
feel. Okay?

Tamira's Child: Okay.

Tamira's Adult: How do you feel now?

Tamira's Child: I still feel a little full and scared of being fat, but I feel
a lot safer now and not so angry. I don't want to die
anymore. When I was little, Mom never let me grieve
Papa's loss. Now I've got to do it, or else I'm never
going to stop being the ice queen. They taught me how
to control and deny my feelings, but that wasn't me.

Tamira's Adult: This is opening a fountain inside. I'm so proud of your
courage.

Tamira's Child: Thanks, Mom. I couldn't do it without you.

Tamira's Adult: I love you. Sweet dreams.

Tamira's Child: Go easy on the food, Mom, please.

Tamira's Adult: Okay. I love you.

Obesity is similar to bulimia in that the Inner Child is using food as
a way to fill the emptiness and avoid feeling alone, but the difference
is that the fat itself also serves a purpose. The Child may use fat to keep
people away so he or she doesn't have to face fears of rejection or
domination. Or the fat may protect the Child from difficult feelings
concerning sexuality. Women who were sexually abused as children
may use fat this way. The Inner Child may have many reasons for
wanting to be fat, even though consciously the person may say he or
she wants to be thin. Even when people manage to lose weight, they
generally gain it back and continue to struggle with their weight until
their Adult begins to nurture their Inner Child.

Anxiety Disorders

Anxiety disorders, such as panic attacks with or without agoraphobia, and simple phobias such as fear of flying, of heights, of snakes or dogs, are also common in our society. Panic attacks occur when the Inner Child encounters a situation that triggers its feelings of intense fear or aloneness and has no Adult to nurture, support, and handle the situation. Panic attacks often occur when the Inner Child feels trapped into betraying itself to avoid rejection or trapped in a situation where it believes it can't safely get out.

Karen is a woman in her early forties. She has suffered from panic attacks on and off since her early twenties, when she first married. After divorcing her first husband she did not experience panic attacks until a few years after marrying her second husband. Bruce, her present husband, is a typical nice guy, emotionally remote but outwardly caring. Her family has often told her how lucky she is to have found him. When she entered therapy she did not understand why she often experienced panic attacks when she was out with her husband and other people. She is also a public speaker. She did not understand why she sometimes experienced panic attacks before a speech.

In therapy, Karen discovered that when she was out with her husband and other people, her husband would often say and do things that embarrassed her, but because her Adult did not find a way to handle the situation, her Child would feel trapped and immobilized and go into a panic. She also discovered that before giving a speech her Child would be afraid that she would lose her voice, and her Adult would never comfort her or tell her the truth—that she never had lost her voice, and even if she did nothing bad would happen. People wouldn't hate her, they would understand. Without her Adult telling her the truth, Karen's Inner Child was left alone with her fear and would panic.

As Karen's loving Adult learned to comfort her Inner Child, her panic attacks subsided. This took awhile, because Karen was afraid to know how her Child felt about Bruce. She had to be willing to lose the relationship before she was able to reach her Child. Sure enough, she discovered that she really didn't like Bruce at all, that she was very bored with him and his remoteness, and that her Child felt trapped in the marriage. Her Child's panic went away when Karen reassured her Child that she was not trapped, that she could leave if things didn't work out, but that first Karen wanted to try marriage counseling.

Agoraphobia has the same root cause. The Inner Child is too frightened to be out alone, especially in crowds. It may have hidden memories of abuse or molestation that occurred in crowds, or memories of having been lost or actually left by a parent. There may be fears of humiliation and fears of the panic itself. The Inner Child learns to fear the fear itself, because it is so alone in the fear. When the person's loving Adult learns to comfort the Inner Child, it will no longer fear the fear; it will also be able to heal the past trauma that created the fear.

As little children we often felt unable to control our choices and our lives. If this experience was intense enough, it can result in phobias in adult life, when the Inner Adult is unable to give the Inner Child a feeling of control over his or her own life. The phobias are a projection outward of the inner fear. For example, a fear of being out of control can show up as a fear of flying or a fear of driving on the freeway. A fear of snakes can be a projection of the fear of a person. For example, a woman might fear snakes if the snake has become symbolic of a father who sexually abused her. When the Adult is able to help the Child separate snakes from father and help the Child to express her fear and pain about her father, then the fear can be healed.

Depression

Depression occurs when the Adult *depresses* the Child's aliveness and energy by discounting and ignoring its wants and needs. A person may be depressed about a job that the Child hates and that the Adult has taken no steps to change. The Adult is acting as if the Child doesn't exist, and this causes the Child to be depressed. A person may be depressed when he or she remains in a relationship that the Child doesn't want to be in. If a person stays in a relationship "for the children" or because he or she is afraid to leave, then the Child feels trapped and depressed. It's amazing how fast depression goes away when the Adult is willing to hear the Child and act in its behalf.

Nathan is a very successful architect who has suffered from periodic bouts of depression for which he has had to be hospitalized. While Nathan has been very connected to his Inner Child in his work, which is why he is so successful, he has often ignored his Child in personal situations. Whenever he has ignored the signals from his Child, he has ended up in a severe depression. His Child feels so frightened when Adult Nathan abandons him that the fear triggers a chemical reaction in Nathan's body that puts him into a severe depression. Since Nathan has learned to listen to his inner signals and act accordingly, his depressions have ceased.

Group Therapy

You might find that you gain more from working in a group than working individually. Experiencing others going through their own processes can help you become aware of areas in which you need to work. Seeing others accept their own deep anger, pain, and fear and move through them can give you the courage to do the same. You may receive a great deal of support from the other group members, as well as learning how to offer the truth as you see it in a loving and compassionate way. Group therapy can help heal feelings of isolation and disconnection in the presence of others. The honesty and caring in a group create a sense of connection with others that you may never have experienced. Group therapy, unfortunately, is often inappropriate for people suffering from personality disorders. The Inner Child feels so threatened and is so disruptive in groups that such a person is best helped individually.

The following will give you a taste of the kind of growth that can happen in a women's group. Watch for the insights and questions from the different women and notice how the group's contributions help Sarah do her work—and how much she brings in from her own work outside of group. Therapy groups can be a very exciting place to learn.

Sarah: [Black-haired, blue-eyed Sarah is in her mid-thirties and is very short—maybe 4 feet 11 inches tall. She has a two-year-old son and is recently divorced.] I want to talk about my weight. I haven't brought this up before. I gained a lot of weight when I had my baby and then afterwards I had a lot of physical problems. When I divorced Jeremy, a major problem was his telling me that I was ugly and fat and ordering me to lose weight. I went to a diet center, but I couldn't lose it. I was one of those cases where it stays on for a reason: even though you're dieting and doing everything in the program, you still don't lose weight. They talked about how you can hang on to the weight mentally. When Jeremy and I got into mediation, I lost a lot of weight. I notice that I've gained some back instead of continuing the loss. I know there's a reason, something inside of me that I'm really out of touch with. All the way over here today, part of me was saying, "You should talk about this, you should work on this." Because now I really want to work on this, now I really want to lose the weight. I want to get my body in shape. I need to learn about what is going on with me.

Margie: What does your Child feel?

Sarah's Child: Yeah. Oh, wow. I needed it to protect me. I hurt so bad. I needed it to be stronger and not be attacked so much.

Margie: Do you need it to protect you because the Adult Sarah hasn't been there to protect you?

Sarah's Child: I don't know. I just haven't felt strong.

Linda: Do you feel out there alone?

Sarah's Child: I don't feel alone. She's here, but she hasn't been strong enough to protect me, she's been just trying to take care of so much stuff. I just didn't think I could do it all. I didn't think I could do it all if I wasn't bigger, physically bigger. And that's it. Just bigger. Just trying to be . . . not so little. Not so little. I just don't want to be run over. Wow. (Her voice shifts to a deeper, calmer, very soft Adult place.) I love you.

Julie: Who are you saying I love you to?

Sarah's Adult: Myself. I love you. I need comforting and I'm comforting myself. It's me—just being bigger and stronger.

Margie: Your Child believes that bigness is in your physical size?

Sarah: Yeah.

Margie: Not in your emotional strength?

Sarah: Yeah. I realize that. I see that. And I know that isn't true, but that's what's been going on. It's so amazing how this stuff comes up! It's so amazing. I had a flash that it isn't physical strength at all, but an energy strength, this core of energy strength deep within me that I need to strengthen. I'd never realized that before. I never felt that way before. I never gained weight to be bigger before.

Linda: Maybe you never had to be that strong before.

Sarah: Never had to be that strong before . . . That's right. That's really amazing.

Megan: Do you feel more protected in terms of Jeremy when you have this weight around you? Sexually?

Sarah: Yeah.

Susanna: Like when you were pregnant?

Sarah: Actually, being pregnant was very safe. He didn't harass me.

Marcia: Was he abusive?

Sarah: Yuck. I don't want to talk about that. He was a sexual addict. But I did feel safe the whole time I was pregnant with Dylan. We were married such a short time before I got pregnant, really. And he was really very seductive until I got pregnant. So I did use weight that way, to protect me against him too. And I guess I'm still doing it. Not sexually, though. The great thing is I'm learning to confront him, to stand up with my truth about what's happening and let that do it. Let my truth protect me. And that's working. I've seen it working. It's so weird. Now he's getting friendly toward me again. You know, seductive with me again. It's so weird. He's been this way twice now. It makes me feel really weird. Maybe that's why I'm starting to gain weight again, too.

Megan: I was going to ask you about that.

Sarah: I just realized that right now! That's so weird, because the last couple of times I saw him, he almost kissed me.

Megan: So maybe being thin means being vulnerable to him.

Sarah: Definitely.

Margie: But that would be true only if the Adult you is not protecting the Child.

Sarah: Right. And that's what I've seen. I realize that. I really feel like it's right on when we talk about Jeremy trying to get close to me again and me using that as a way to distance myself from him and protect myself from the world because my Adult hasn't been there for me.

Margie: So it seems that it's all connected to the Adult not taking care of the Child and the Child needing to find a way to feel safe. If Jeremy tried to kiss you, the loving Adult would hear the Child saying, "This doesn't feel good" and would respond by saying *"No"* to Jeremy. But if the Adult doesn't do that, then the Child needs to protect somehow.

Megan: Yes. So your fat is helping you say no, instead of you saying no.

Sarah: Yeah, I can really see it. And I think it started with that betrayal we talked about last week, of myself and my Child. Because I knew before I married him that the relationship was abusive to me, wasn't good for me, and I didn't listen to myself. I wasn't there for myself.

Margie: Do you feel angry about it?

Sarah: I know there is an element of anger there for sure, but it feels more like what we've already zeroed in on. It's a protection, a distancing from the sexual stuff and the power stuff.

Susanna: I was curious when Marcia asked you if he had been abusive and you just snapped at her and said, "I don't want to work on that!" And now when Margie mentioned the anger, you're saying that anger doesn't fit for you . . .

Sarah: Well, I just spent a lot of time with that at home and it didn't seem to fit me. Are you trying to get me in touch with my anger?

Susanna: Remember I said last week I'm feeling anger towards Jeremy, so maybe it's my issue! He was abusive, and I'm angry at him for abusing you the way he did.

Sarah: Yeah. Okay. There's a belief. I just saw a belief. I realized that I don't want the anger to debilitate me. For a long time I've been so angry that it had a debilitating effect on me. I've been working on letting it go. I work on this every night. My little Child and I talk about this and cry about it and try to release it. I write affirmations over and over again, treatments about releasing this anger and not letting it destroy me.

Susanna: But I've never seen you feel the anger.

Sarah: I have felt the anger but I've never shared it here. It's so over-whelming. It's like screaming. It *is* screaming. (She starts to cry.) It's so much! It's so much!

Margie: It sounds like you feel you're going to burden people if you let them have your anger.

Sarah: Yes. Yeah, because it's so much!

Margie: Why wouldn't you want to unburden yourself here?

Sarah: I don't know. I just want to let it go!

Megan: The burden is the holding it in!

Susanna: Remember when I worked in here a couple of sessions ago? That was the belief I had about my rage toward Gene [her ex-boyfriend]. And what I've learned in group is that I have to be angry and I have to let it out, even though I'm frightened to let everybody else experience it. I thought it would be too scary, or I was too ashamed of it. I had to let it out. I had to *be* angry. I had to feel what it was like to be that victim before I could be at peace with it. It's like you're skipping a step. Or you're trying to do it in the quiet of your own home alone in bed and crying.

Sarah: Well, I punch things out and stuff . . .

Margie: I don't think doing it alone is the same thing.

Julie: Sometimes you need a witness to validate it.

Marcia: You want to try it? (gives her a batacca—a foam bat designed to hit and release anger) Put him on the floor.

Sarah: Well, I *do* hate him. I think that a lot when I talk to him, too. I get off the phone and I say, "I hate your guts, you asshole. You're fucked." He is very manipulative. (She gets down off her chair and kneels on the floor.)

Margie: See him leering at you.

Sarah: Oh God, Margie! (She cries, softly and weakly. The words come out haltingly, tentatively.) I really, really hate you. I really hate you. You didn't even try and you hurt me so bad. And you didn't even try. You didn't even care.

Margie: Sarah, start to hit him. Just start. Let the strength come up. Let the anger come up.

Sarah: (not moving, bent over) I feel really stupid. I feel ashamed.

Margie: You aren't giving your Child a chance. You're telling her she's stupid.

Sarah: I know. I'm gonna get there. I'm gonna get there.

Margie: Imagine if your son were angry and you told him he was stupid for his anger.

Sarah: No, I wouldn't do that.

Margie: That's what you're doing with your Child right now; you're telling her that she's stupid. She has a lot of anger and she has a right to it. She needs a voice to express it. She is enraged at him.

Sarah: (still softly and tentatively) You raped me and I hate you.

Margie: Start hitting.

Sarah: I hate you. I hate you. I hate you. I hate you.

Margie: Louder.

Sarah: I hate you. I hate you. I hate you. I hate you. I hate you. I hate you. I hate you. I hate what you did to me. (Sarah begins to hit and experience her rage.) I hate you.

Margie: Louder, Sarah.

Sarah: (She gets louder, puts even more energy into it.) *I hate you. I hate you. I hate you. I hate you. I hate you.*

Margie: (even louder) **I hate you.**

Sarah: (Screaming for all she's worth, beating rhythmically but without conviction, about one hit per second.) I hate you. I hate you. I hate you. I hate you. (Throat contracting, she resorts to wordless sounds coming up from her belly as she pounds the floor.) Auuuugh. (hit) Auuugh. (hit)

Margie: Use your whole body. Hit him with all your strength. Let your anger come into you like a rod through you and really give it to him!

Sarah: (Starts to cough. Three or four hits with only coughing behind the muscle. Same rhythm on the hits.) Auugh. (hit) Auuugh. (hit) (She really starts to choke.) Oooooh. Ooooh. Oh God. Oooooh.

Margie: Sarah, I want you to be aware of the blockage in your cough. The coughing is how you are blocking the true free flow of this. It's like your Child wants to get out more than anything, but the Adult is saying, "No, it's too much, it's too much." You can't go all the way with this because you're still putting a limit on yourself.

Sarah: Yeah.

Margie: You're telling your Child, "That's enough, that's enough. Don't go too far with this!"

Sarah: I'm really scared.

Susanna: Why? What are you scared of?

Sarah: (starts to cry again) I'm just really afraid of losing it and not being able to deal with Dylan or anything right now. I have to pick him up at day care and be okay.

Margie: Sarah, everybody in here will be sure that you leave here in one piece, okay?

Sarah: Okay, okay, I'll do it again.

Margie: Let yourself fall apart. Make it okay to fall apart. Go all the way to the bottom.

Sarah: Okay. (to Susanna, at her side) You better get back. All right. I'm gonna take off my watch. Okay. I'm just really scared.

Margie: That's okay. Tell your Child that you have all sorts of people here to take care of her. It's okay for her to fall apart.

Sarah: (to herself, softly) It's okay. It's okay. It's okay.

Margie: She can completely fall apart.

Sarah: Okay. Okay.

Linda: And she can say she's scared as many times as she wants to.

Sarah's Child: Okay. (She takes a few deep breaths and gets into her rage fully, hitting with more power and faster—about three hits in two seconds.) Ungh. Ungh. Ungh. ARRRRRRGH! (a primal scream, starting from her toes and coming up her whole body) ARRRRRRRRGH! (a second scream, deep as the first) **I HATE YOU! I HATE YOU! I HATE YOU! YOU HURT ME SO BAD! YOU'RE AWFUL! YOU'RE AWFUL! YOU'RE AWFUL! I HATE YOU! I HATE YOU! YOU BASTARD! YOU HURT ME SO BAD! YOU HURT ME SO BAD! I DON'T DESERVE WHAT YOU DID! I HATE YOU! I COULDN'T SAY NO! I . . . HATE . . . YOU! I HATE YOU! I HATE YOU! AUUUUUUUGH. AT THE START YOU WEREN'T THERE. YOU WEREN'T THERE FOR ME! YOU . . . WEREN'T THERE . . . FOR ME! YOU WEREN'T THERE . . . AND NO ONE HELPED ME! NO ONE PROTECTED ME! AND NO ONE WAS THERE FOR ME! YOU HURT ME SO BAD!** (She starts to cry.) **YOU . . . HURT ME . . . SO BAD . . .** (She gasps for breath, exhausted. The hitting stops as she stays bent over, crying and trying to catch her breath.) I hate you. I hate you. (Heavy breathing for about forty-five seconds, as Sarah reintegrates and assesses what has just happened.) God. I am so angry at myself.

Margie: Put yourself there, in front of you to hit. Put your Adult self there and let the Child speak to her.

Sarah's Child: Yes. (quietly, numbly) You weren't there for me, and you let him do all that to me. I hate you for doing that. You didn't love me and you have never loved me. You've always hurt me. In all the years and everything. You never cared.

Sarah: Wow. I didn't know that. I hated me.

Margie: Talk to your Child.

Sarah's Adult: I love you. I am very sorry. I hurt you. I hurt you. I hurt you. I'm the one that hurt you. Besides him. I really let it happen and I didn't say no. I didn't think it was okay to say no. I'm sorry. I'm really sorry. I'll do it now. I'm taking care of you now. I'm doing good with you now. I love you. And I won't abandon you. Wow! Wow! I had no idea how much I had down there. I love you. I really love you. You're very special. Very special.

Margie: Will you tell her how you understand that she's needed to be overweight because of you?

Sarah's Adult: I understand how you've needed to protect yourself and I've just let you do it. I've encouraged it and not really helped you be powerful without it. I know you don't need to do that anymore, because I'll be with you to help you. This is a lot. This is really a lot.

Margie: You don't look like you're falling apart.

Sarah: No, you're right. I'm not. I feel much better.

Margie: So I want you to really look at that belief. It is truly a false belief that if you go to the bottom of your rage you will fall apart.

Sarah: Yeah, it is.

Margie: That is not what happens.

Sarah: You know, I get that from my mom. She believed that too. That stoic stuff.

Megan: Sarah, I want to say how moved I am. I'm so glad you were able to do this. It is such a big, a monumental step and I'm really happy for you. I really admire you for doing it.

Linda: How brave you are, for moving along so much so fast.

Sarah: Well, you know it's amazing. My Child really wants to work it out; she wants to be heard. I think all the way over here today, the weight issue was just pounding in my mind. I didn't know how to bring it up or what exactly to say, but it doesn't really matter, because it came. All right. Let's move along! Someone else's turn.

Margie: That's a relief. When someone really goes to the bottom of that rage . . .

Sarah: Yeah, it feels like quite a release.

The following week Sarah worked again. She told the group that when she was twelve she burned her hand and spent some time in a hospital. One day when no nurses were around she read her hospital records and discovered that she was not actually there for her hand but because she was too emotionally upset for her mother to take care of; she ripped the dressings off her burn every night and had to be tied to the bed. So Sarah decided that her emotional pain was unacceptable and shut it down from then on. The week after that she had some more insights:

Sarah: I had this big breakthrough last week. I realized something from my childhood. I was really drugged in my childhood. I was given Nembutol, which is a very heavy-duty drug, when I burned my hand. They gave my mother a huge bottle of it and told her to give it to me whenever I felt pain. So she gave it to me every time I felt any *emotional* pain. I really learned from that. I mean, I'm not an alcoholic or a drug addict, but I drink Coca-Cola when I feel really upset. I've learned to suppress my feelings with drugs like caffeine. I don't like alcohol much at all.

Margie: And you smoke, don't you?

Sarah: I've been smoking lately.

Margie: So that's another drug.

Sarah: Oh definitely. It's an oral thing. And I just wanted to tell the group that after last week I realized I'd been doing that.

Susanna: What about food?

Sarah: Maybe I have . . . Yes, since I had the baby, since I was with Jeremy, I have used food.

Margie: Because food and caffeine and nicotine work very well to suppress feelings.

Sarah: That's right. And my Child really wanted to say that to the group today, to confess it. It was a major insight for me after last week. And I met this incredible guy who I'll be working with. He's the first insightful, intuitive man I've met. I had him over to my house the other night for a meeting and I was so-o-o-o nervous. I'm even nervous now, talking about it. And I had wine and I had cigarettes. I really noticed that. So I stopped doing that yesterday. Well, it's a beginning. I stopped smoking and drinking and taking things into my body.

Emily: Wow, just like that? That's great!

Sarah: I mean, I'm talking about smoking a couple of cigarettes at night. It's not like I'm chain smoking, but now I can see why I was doing it. Because at night is when my feelings come up for the most part. I just don't want to drug my Child anymore. That's what it's been more than anything, realizing how I learned to do that. Like finally seeing that false belief that emotions are too much, that you have to suppress them and use some kind of chemical or food, like you said. Food is a new one. I knew Coca-Cola, because when I was really upset my mom used to give me Coke and I liked that. I learned that. So I'm not going to do that anymore. That's all. It's amazing. I started to talk about that guy and I started shaking. Isn't that amazing?

Margie: Why?

Sarah: (crying) Because I was so scared, being around someone. I mean, work I can do, but I definitely felt something for this person. Something just nice, not extremely lustful, although some of it was lustful. But it was just that it's possible that there is a man who's somewhat like me—you know, intuitive and not a fucking asshole who wants to hurt me. Like a really nice woman friend that I trust. I like this guy. It's just amazing how I smoked. I was really aware of how I was using it to distance myself from him and the situation, so we'd really focus on the work instead.

Margie: I wonder if you've talked to your Child from your Adult? Have you told her that there is no such thing as your feelings being too much or too intense?

Sarah: I've been saying that a lot to her. Like last night, I deliberately didn't do anything—I didn't smoke a cigarette, I didn't have coffee or tea or Coke or eat anything that I felt would take away from her feelings. I was really talking with her about the fact that our emotions are not too much. My whole history taught me that emotions were too much, that you should suppress them and not show them to people. And last night was the final thing I could do to let my little girl know that. Because she has been screaming inside, "You've been dosing me!" whenever I've had these extreme emotions come up and I've used something. Something that may be socially acceptable, nothing too radical, but it's been just extreme for her. So I feel really good about that and that was the first time since I was twelve. That was when I really learned to do it, when they sedated me for so long while I was healing. There was pain with my hand, but it was really emotional pain that I learned to suppress. So mainly it's an ongoing process with me and I wanted to share that with the group.

Margie: Incredible decision. Really powerful.

Sarah: Yeah. It's a really big decision. I don't even want a cigarette or anything right now. I feel as if she's at peace within me about it.

Couple Therapy

Couples come into therapy for a variety of reasons—they're fighting all the time, or bored with each other, or one has just found out that the other is having an affair, or they have no sex life, or they can't talk to each other. Each is generally very aware of what the *other* is doing that is causing the problems and very unaware of their own contribution to the problem. They each experience themselves as reactors to the other. "I wouldn't get so angry if she wanted sex more often." "I wouldn't have to nag if he was more responsible around the house." "I wouldn't get so mad if he would pay attention to me once in a while." "I'd feel more like talking if she weren't such a bitch." On and on, blaming the other for his or her own choices: a codependent relationship.

In order for such a relationship to grow and become loving, each partner must be willing to do his or her own inner work. Sometimes they can learn to do this together in the therapy sessions, but sometimes they need individual therapy. If one or both partners are very angry, blaming, or shut down, joint sessions do not work. Each needs to do his or her own work until they can be supportive of each other's inner process. Then they can work together in session.

If one partner has decided to come for therapy to work on himself or herself, it is often helpful if the other partner will come for a few sessions. A client may seem very open in the therapy office alone, but may change totally when the partner is there. Sometimes the depth of a codependent system does not show up unless the therapist can witness their interaction.

Sherrill came in for therapy because her husband Roger was always running around with other women. Sherrill was a beautiful, talented, highly intelligent woman, who appeared to be very open, loving, and aware. It was difficult to see Sherrill's role in creating the problem, other than the fact that she was staying in the relationship and hoping Roger would change. But the therapist knew that, as with all couples, both partners had created the problem. Fortunately, Roger was willing to come in for a few sessions. The therapist was amazed to see what happened to Sherrill in Roger's presence. Her Adult just disappeared. She became a whining and manipulative little girl, using her seductiveness to attempt to control him. She lied to him in front of the therapist and was extremely distant emotionally. Roger reacted to this with anger, which frightened Sherrill into total silence. It quickly became apparent to the therapist that both of these people were abandoned Children with each other, each acting out in their own ways. With the therapist's help, Sherrill and Roger could see this, too. They decided to each work on themselves in individual therapy and to have joint sessions every two weeks. As they each learn how to respond to each other as their Adult and how to connect with their Inner Child, their relationship is becoming more loving and connected.

CHAPTER 13

Making the Commitment

We go back . . . and back . . . and back . . . through the layers of
fear, shame, rage, hurt, and negative incantations until we discover
the exuberant, unencumbered, delightful, and lovable child that
was, and still is, in us.

And once we find it, we love and cherish it, and never, never
let it go.

Beyond Codependence
MELODY BEATTIE

You would never think of showing up for a piano recital without having practiced the piano every day for months and reached a point
where you felt you could play even under pressure. If you were a
surgeon, you would not think of performing major surgery until you
had practiced over and over and felt you could handle a crisis situation.
Being a loving Adult for your Inner Child when it is afraid takes a lot
of practice. We know from our own experiences and the experiences of
our clients that the dialoguing creates loving inner connection, but it
works only if you *do* it. Too often people read a book like this and
understand the concepts and think that because they have understood,
a change will take place. *Change will take place only if you make the commitment to practice daily.*

Staying lovingly connected in the face of fear is the challenge. Some
people function in a loving connected way part of the time, but disconnect as soon as they experience fear—fear of rejection, of being
out of control, of domination, failure, pain, anger, humiliation, or
loneliness. Yet this is when your Inner Child most needs you as a
loving Adult. You will not be able to do this consistently unless you
practice connecting with your Inner Child lovingly and learn what it
means to be there for your Child's fear.

You will not find the peace and happiness you are looking for unless you are truly *devoted to your own joy.* We sometimes refer to this in
therapy as working on your joy instead of working on your issues.
How many of you can honestly say that you are devoted to your joy,

to discovering what truly makes you happy and acting to bring that about? Most people, if they are honest with themselves, are devoted to feeling safe, to avoiding pain, to being loved. You will not discover your joy until you are willing to choose risks over safety, to learn from your pain rather than avoid it, and you want to be loving more than you want to be loved.

One of our clients exclaimed, upon grasping the concept of the Inner Adult/Inner Child connection, "Is that what it means to be a 'together' person?" Yes! A "together" person is an integrated person, a person with a sense of inner harmony and inner balance, a person who functions in the world from a place of personal power. These people are inwardly connected, though they may not be able to explain it in these terms. All of us have the option of being "together" within ourselves, but it takes the Adult's deep commitment to learn with and from the Inner Child.

The Bible speaks of "the fall," meaning the fall away from God, and states that this is the original sin. We can use this as a metaphor to symbolize the fall away from ourselves, from our Inner Child. We can see paradise as the connection between the Inner Adult and the Inner Child, which leads to wholeness, to the Higher Self, and to connection with universal God/Goddess love and consciousness. When we disconnect from ourselves and look for comfort and approval from outside of ourselves (the apple) rather than seeking them within, we move into a state of denial—denial of our inner awareness, and we fall from grace. This truly is our original sin, a sin against ourselves, against our own Inner Child, a sin that we each have the power to heal by making a commitment to learn.

As we open ourselves to learning, we inevitably confront the question, "What is our purpose in life? Why are we here? What's it all about?" We would like to share with you our personal answer to this question. Our purpose is to clear away whatever blocks us from being totally loving human beings. Our immediate purpose is to be loving to our Inner Child, for then we will automatically be loving to others. By becoming fully loving human beings, by that and nothing else, we will help to heal the planet. We believe that we are all here to learn how to be loving human beings and thereby help to heal the planet. We believe that whatever we do that brings us joy and that helps us evolve into more loving people is another step toward healing the planet. We believe that our consciousness affects the consciousness of others and affects the collective consciousness, and that all of us are here for that same purpose. All this gives a tremendous amount of meaning to our lives, because it affects everything we do. If we are playing joyfully, we are adding joy to the world. If we're painting and putting our own experience onto the canvas so other people can experience it, or if we're writing music, or writing books, and the process brings us joy, then we're adding something to the world. If we're doing therapy and we're helping people become more loving, then we're adding to the world, but only if the process itself brings us joy. If we're alone and taking care of our Inner Child in some way, playing solitaire, reading, boating, meditating, creating, and feeling a sense of peace, we are adding to the peacefulness of the world.

Our reason for being here—to become pure love, to become one with the universal God/Goddess energy of love and truth—is always with us. The love we express affects the world. As each person expresses more love the world is affected profoundly. But we cannot make other people move toward that goal; we do not have that kind of control. We can only move toward it ourselves.

When you let what is loving to yourself be your guide, when you "follow your bliss," then you stay connected and in your Higher Self, because that is how you are guided. If a relationship, or a job, or a behavior is not loving to yourself, does not bring you peace or joy, then it is not loving to the planet. No matter what else happens, that is central. That is what gives us the courage to move ahead and do what we have to do, even though it may be frightening to move out of a relationship, or change jobs, or behave differently. As we begin to love our Inner Child, we heal ourselves. As we heal ourselves, we heal the world.

Suggested Reading

Bass, Ellen, and Laura Davis. *The Courage to Heal* (New York: Harper & Row, 1988).
Extremely helpful in opening to memories of childhood abuse and in understanding the healing process.

Beattie, Melody. *Beyond Codependence* (San Francisco: Harper & Row, 1989).

———. *Codependent No More: How to Stop Controlling Others and Start Caring for Yourself* (San Francisco: Harper & Row, 1987).

Bradshaw, John. *The Family* (Deerfield Beach, FL: Health Communications, 1988).
Shows how the inner disconnection begins and gets handed down through the family.

———. *Healing the Shame That Binds You* (Deerfield Beach, FL: Health Communications, 1988).
Helpful in understanding the feelings of the abandoned Inner Child.

Dyer, Wayne. *Your Erroneous Zones* (New York: Avon, 1977).
Helpful in dealing with false beliefs.

Eisler, Riane. *The Chalice and the Blade* (San Francisco: Harper & Row, 1987).
A wonderful book that helps us understand the origins of disconnection within our history. Shows us how we got onto the wrong path.

Fynn. *Mr. God, This is Anna* (New York: Ballantine, 1974).
A wonderful example of a child who never abandoned herself.

Forward, Susan. *Toxic Parents* (New York: Bantam, 1989).
Excellent in becoming aware of the source of our unloving inner parenting, and in helping us to heal.

Gendlin, Eugene T. *Focusing* (New York: Bantam, 1978).
Very helpful in learning to tune in to your feelings.

Jeffers, Susan. *Feel the Fear and Do It Anyway* (New York: Harcourt Brace Jovanovich, 1987).
Helpful in understanding what it means to face fear, especially fear of pain, and move beyond it.

Kaufman, Barry Neil. *To Love Is to Be Happy With* (New York: Coward, McCann and Goeghegan, 1977).

Helpful in learning how to ask your Inner Child questions.

Liefloff, Jean. *The Continuum Concept: Allowing Human Nature to Work Successfully* (Reading, MA: Addison Wesley, 1977).
In our opinion, this is one of the most important books ever written. She offers us a look into a society where loving parenting and resulting loving self-parenting actually exists.

Miller, Alice. *Thou Shalt Not Be Aware: Psychoanalysis and Society's Betrayal of the Child* (New York: Farrar, Straus and Giroux, 1984).

———. *For Your Own Good: Hidden Cruelty in Child-Rearing and the Roots of Violence* (New York: Farrar, Straus and Giroux, 1983).

Paul, Jordan and Margaret. *From Conflict to Caring* (Minneapolis: CompCare, 1989).
Filled with questions to ask yourself and exercises to help you explore your fears and false beliefs.

———. *If You Really Loved Me* (Minneapolis: CompCare, 1987).
This book not only provides a role model for loving parenting, but for loving self-parenting as well. Helpful in understanding the intent to learn with real-life children and with your Inner Child.

———. *Do I Have to Give Up Me to be Loved by You?* (Minneapolis: CompCare, 1983).
For a detailed understanding of the intent to protect and the intent to learn and how they apply in relationships.

Schaef, Anne Wilson. *Escape from Intimacy* (San Francisco: Harper & Row, 1989).
Helpful in understanding addiction to relationships, love, and romance.

———. *When Society Becomes an Addict* (San Francisco: Harper & Row, 1988).

Dr. Margaret Paul is a psychotherapist and author who has maintained a private practice in West Los Angeles for the past twenty years. Margaret's parenting skills have been honed by raising three children, ages 24, 21, and 18. She has taught at several colleges and has conducted workshops all across the United States. Her chief avocation is painting.

Dr. Erika Chopich is a psychotherapist and author who maintains a private practice in West Los Angeles and lectures throughout the United States. Her work background—paramedic, dental administration, union negotiator, professional chef, and restauranteur—is as varied as her play interests—boating, fishing, soaring, and model railroading.